tasty tomato
cookbook

tasty tomato cookbook

mouthwatering meals using a classic ingredient

christine france

southwater

This edition is published by Southwater

Southwater is an imprint of Anness Publishing Ltd
Hermes House, 88–89 Blackfriars Road, London SE1 8HA
tel. 020 7401 2077; fax 020 7633 9499
www.southwaterbooks.com; info@anness.com

© Anness Publishing Ltd 2003

This edition distributed in the UK by The Manning Partnership Ltd, tel. 01225 478 444; fax 01225 478 440; sales@manning-partnership.co.uk

This edition distributed in the USA and Canada by National Book Network, tel. 301 459 3366; fax 301 459 1705; www.nbnbooks.com

This edition distributed in Australia by Pan Macmillan Australia, tel. 1300 135 113; fax 1300 135 103; customer.service@macmillan.com.au

This edition distributed in New Zealand by The Five Mile Press (NZ) Ltd, tel. (09) 444 4144; fax (09) 444 4518; fivemilenz@clear.net.nz

All rights reserved. No part of this publication may be reproduced, stored in a retrieval system, or transmitted in any way or by any means, electronic, mechanical, photocopying, recording or otherwise, without the prior written permission of the copyright holder.

A CIP catalogue record for this book is available from the British Library.

Publisher: Joanna Lorenz
Managing Editors: Linda Fraser, Helen Sudell
Project Editor: Jennifer Schofield
Production Controller: Claire Rae
Designer: Juliet Brown, Axis Design
Additional text: Jenni Fleetwood, Richard Bird
Recipes: Catherine Atkinson, Alex Barker, Michelle Berriedale-Johnson, Angela Boggiano, Janet Brinkworth, Kathy Brown, Carole Clements, Trish Davies, Patrizia Diemling, Tessa Evelegh, Silvano Franco, Shirley Gill, Brian Glover, Nicola Graimes, Rosamund Grant, Carole Handslip, Shehzad Husain, Christine Ingram, Manisha Kanani, Soheila Kimberley, Lucy Knox, Lesley Mackley, Sally Mansfield, Elizabeth Martin, Norma Miller, Jane Milton, Sallie Morris, Elisabeth Lambert Ortiz, Maggie Pannell, Anne Sheasby, Liz Trigg, Elizabeth Wolf-Cohen, Jeni Wright
Photography: Karl Adamson, Edward Allwright, David Armstrong, Steve Baxter, James Duncan, Ian Garlick, Michelle Garrett, Amanda Heywood, Janine Hosegood, David Jordan, Dave King, Don Last, William Lingwood, Patrick McLeavey, Steve Moss, Thomas Odulate, Craig Robertson, Simon Smith, Sam Stowell

Previously published as part of a larger compendium, *Tomato*.

1 3 5 7 9 10 8 6 4 2

NOTES
Bracketed terms are intended for American readers.

For all recipes, quantities are given in both metric and imperial measures and, where appropriate, measures are also given in standard cups and spoons.
Follow one set, but not a mixture, because they are not interchangeable.

Standard spoon and cup measures are level.
1 tsp = 5ml, 1 tbsp = 15ml, 1 cup = 250ml/8fl oz

Australian standard tablespoons are 20ml. Australian readers should use 3 tsp in place of 1 tbsp for measuring small quantities of gelatine, flour, salt, etc.

Medium (US large) eggs are used unless otherwise stated.

CONTENTS

THE TALE OF THE TOMATO	6
CULTIVATING TOMATOES	10
GUIDE TO BUYING TOMATOES	12
USEFUL EQUIPMENT	14
PREPARING TOMATOES	16
PRESERVING TOMATOES	18
TOMATOES IN THE PANTRY	19
THE TASTIER TOMATO	20
GUIDE TO TOMATO VARIETIES	22

SOUPS AND SNACKS	30
SIDE DISHES AND SALADS	52
MEAT AND POULTRY	76
FISH AND SHELLFISH	94
VEGETARIAN MAIN MEALS	112
SALSAS, RELISHES AND DIPS	142
INDEX	158

The Tale of the Tomato

The early history of the tomato is not clear, but it is thought that the first known tomatoes grew wild in South America, to the west of the Andes in what is now Peru, Bolivia, northern Chile and Ecuador. The ancestors of the Incas and Aztecs were the first to cultivate the tiny, cherry-sized fruits around 700AD.

Both the Aztecs and the Mayas farmed the little fruits for food, and their cultivation began to spread. By the time the Spaniards conquered Mexico in the early 16th century, tomatoes were widely domesticated there and throughout South America.

There is little doubt that we have the Spanish to thank for bringing tomatoes to Europe. Tradition has it that a Spanish priest returning from Peru brought the first seeds back to Seville, but, in reality, it seems more likely to have been a Spanish explorer: perhaps Christopher Columbus or Hernando Cortés. Many acknowledge Cortés as the person who brought the tomato to Europe.

Tomato plants would have arrived in Spain by boat, either from the expedition to the New World by Columbus in the 1490s, or brought back by Cortés after the Conquest of Mexico in 1519.

NAMING THE TOMATO

These early tomatoes introduced to Europe would have been small and yellow in colour, not bright red as is common today, and were named "Peruvian apples", or often "golden apples" – "pomo d'oro" in Italian, "pommes d'or" in French, and "Goldapfel" in German.

Either through their supposed aphrodisiac qualities, or because folk medicine linked the appearance of plants to their therapeutic use (tomatoes look very like hearts), they also earned the name of "love apples" or "pommes d'amour", which may also be a simple corruption of "pomo d'oro". Many people believe that the tomato,

Above: Hernando Cortés, 1485–1547, one of the great Spanish explorers, is reputed to have introduced the tomato to Spain after the Conquest of Mexico in the early 16th century.

rather than the apple, was the fruit that Eve used to tempt Adam in the Garden of Eden, and which led to the fall of mankind from grace.

The English word for tomato derives from the original Aztec word "tomatl", but the Latin name "lycopersicon esculentum" translates as "edible wolf's peach" – perhaps reflecting suspicions of its poisonous nature. Indeed, the tomato plant is a member of the deadly nightshade family and the tomato was at first believed to be highly poisonous. In fact, the fruits are not at all toxic, but the foliage is poisonous, and the leaves can cause bad stomach upsets if eaten.

Left: Christopher Columbus, the earliest explorer who may have brought tomatoes to Europe.

Right: Though glasshouses were few and far between in the early 19th century, they were essential for the success of many tomato varieties which could not withstand the cool northern European climates, even in summer. This glasshouse was designed by George Tod in 1812, for Lady Jennings, who lived just outside London.

EARLY CULTIVATION

The tomato was first cultivated in England by John Gerard, who was the superintendent of the College of Physicians' gardens in London. In his book "Gerard's Herball", published in 1597, Gerard described the plant as "of ranke and stinking savour". This unfavourable view of the tomato dominated until the early 19th century in Britain and Northern Europe, and the plants were grown largely as an ornamental curiosity, for their climbing habit, decorative foliage and fruit, or for medicinal use. A poultice of tomato was thought to cure skin disorders, rheumy eyes and the "vapours in women".

Meanwhile, tomatoes flourished in the warm climates of Spain and Italy, and these were the first European nations to realize the potential of tomatoes in cooking, featuring them in recipes from the late 17th century. The early development of new and hardy strains was centred largely around the Mediterranean, and by the mid-18th century there were more than 1,000 tomato varieties, cultivated throughout Spain, Portugal, Italy and the South of France. Eventually the rest of Europe followed suit, helped greatly by the discovery that tomatoes would flourish in glasshouses, extending their season over months instead of weeks. The first glasshouses in England were built in Kent and Essex in the mid-19th century, when sheet glass production was quite a recent innovation.

The North American colonies were also surprisingly cautious about this native fruit, and treated tomatoes with great suspicion when they were reintroduced in the early 1700s.

Some tomato types in cultivation in the 19th century

Though there were many varieties of tomato available, few were cultivated in Europe until the 19th century. Below is a small selection of fruit grown in glasshouses and painted with meticulous accuracy in watercolour paints. They were all included in a cooking ingredients book published in 1879.

Right: cherry-formed red

Right: pear-shaped

Right: cherry-formed yellow

Below: Japanese striped

Above: large red

Above: currant-fruited red

Above: large yellow

Above: rose-fruited red

8 The Tale of the Tomato

It's not certain who was responsible for reintroducing the tomato to North America, but from the mid-18th century, tomatoes were cultivated in Carolina, and by the late 1700s, the migration of farmers across North America took tomato cultivation north and west and to the central coast of Florida. By the early 19th century, tomatoes were widely used in cooking, and recipes reflected the influences of Spanish, Italian, Caribbean or French and other settlers.

THE PRESENT-DAY TOMATO

Once cultivation began on a commercial scale, there was no stopping the tomato. There are now well over 7,000 varieties with new hybrids constantly being introduced.

Tomatoes are grown all over the world, from Iceland to New Zealand. They are one of the main horticultural crops of Britain, about 80 per cent being grown in heated glasshouses, with the rest of the crop being grown almost entirely in unheated greenhouses.

Glasshouses allow the growers to maintain a constant environment for the plants, and provide shelter from inclement weather, as well as consistent water, nutrients and light. This extends the length of the growing season and helps to increase the yield of the plants.

Above: This tomato canning factory still uses hand sorting to choose the best tomatoes. Canned tomatoes have often been ripened on the vine and may have superior flavour to those picked green and artificially ripened for year-round supply to supermarkets.

Above: Markets are one of the best places to buy tomatoes. They are often fresher than those on many supermarket shelves, though the choice may be more seasonal.

Above: Tomato plants being grown on a small commercial scale.

Even when tomatoes are grown on a large scale, bumble-bees are used to pollinate the flowers naturally, and natural predators are used whenever possible in preference to chemicals to control insect damage.

From the day the flowers appear on the tomato plants, it takes between 40 and 60 days for the fruits to reach their peak of ripeness, depending on the tomato variety. If they are grown in coldhouses, the weather will also be a factor. For the finest flavour, tomatoes need to be ripened in the sun and on the vine, and from the first sign of ripening it takes four to six days for a tomato to reach full ripeness.

Commercially, the fruit is picked when it is half-ripened, to allow it to reach the customer when it is at peak ripeness and to extend its shelf-life. Many tomatoes are now sold "on the vine" for aesthetic reasons which allows them to be picked a little later and keep a little bit longer.

Above: Basil is a suitable companion plant for tomatoes.

Below: Even when picked, tomatoes will ripen if left on the vine.

NUTRITION

The nutritional content of tomatoes is important because of the large quantities consumed. Each fruit is between 93 and 95 per cent water, they are a good source of vitamins A and C, and if eaten raw, contain significant amounts of vitamin E. This varies with the variety. Some cherry tomatoes, for instance, contain five times as much vitamin C as other types. Tomatoes also contain a natural bioflavonoid, lycopene. This is a powerful antioxidant that may help to lower the risk of cancer, particularly prostate and colon cancer, and heart disease. Lycopene is a fat-soluble nutrient and is most readily absorbed into the bloodstream when the tomatoes are cooked with a little oil.

Tomatoes also contain potassium, calcium and other mineral salts, and the fibre content is typically around 1.5 per cent. They contain only a trace of fat and just 14 calories/58 kilojoules per 100g/3½oz serving.

Cultivating Tomatoes

Tomatoes are probably the most widely grown of all vegetables. Even people without a garden often manage to grow a plant or two on a balcony or patio, or in a window box. One reason for this is that tomatoes are relatively easy to grow, but another must surely be that supermarket-bought tomatoes sometimes bear little resemblance to what a gardener knows as a tomato. Tomatoes grown at home can be so sweet that they really do live up to their official classification as a fruit, although most people would still consider them a vegetable. Another reason may well be the sheer range of tomatoes that can now be grown at home. They come in all shapes, sizes and colours. Flavours vary, too, and some of the old-fashioned varieties that taste superb are becoming more readily available. The largest, such as the beefsteak tomato, can weigh up to 1.3kg/3lb each, while the smallest are not much bigger than a grape.

Tomatoes can either be grown on cordons (upright plants) or as bushes. It is well worth not only growing your own particular favourite varieties each year, but also experimenting with at least one new one. This may well result in a glut of tomatoes, but they are wonderful

Above: A bed of tomato plants with good exposure to the sun for ripening.

things to give away or they can be made into sauces and frozen for later use. They make very decorative plants, with their red, yellow, green, orange or even purple fruits, and they are a valuable addition to ornamental gardens.

Tomatoes are used widely in raw and cooked dishes. They can even be used in their unripened state, so that any that have not ripened by the time the frosts arrive can still be used.

Tomatoes are half-hardy and can be grown under glass or outside. Growing under glass extends the growing season and results in heavier crops, but outside crops often taste better, particularly if the summer has been hot and the fruit has ripened well.

CULTIVATION IN A GREENHOUSE

If you are growing under glass, sow the seed in mid-spring in a very gentle heat or an unheated greenhouse. An earlier start can be made in a heated greenhouse to obtain earlier crops. When the seedlings are big enough to handle, prick them out into single pots. When the plants are large enough, transfer them to grow bags or a greenhouse border. Arrange some support, such as strings or stakes, for the tomatoes to be tied to as they grow. Remove any side shoots as they appear. Keep well watered and feed every ten days with a high-potash liquid fertilizer once the fruits begin to swell. Pinch out the top of the plant when it reaches the glass.

Above: A satisfying crop.

Above: A greenhouse is ideal for growing old favourites and new varieties.

CULTIVATION OUTDOORS

For cordons grown outside, follow the same procedure as in the greenhouse, but let the plants harden off. This simply means that the plants should be put outside in mild weather during the day for a week or so, before planting out. They should be planted in fertile soil in an open, sunny position. Bush forms are treated in the same way, except that the side shoots do not need to be removed and straw should be placed around the base of the plant to keep the fruit away from the ground.

Cultivation – the facts

Indoors
Sowing time early to mid-spring
Planting time mid- to late spring
Planting/sowing distance 45cm/18in
Harvesting summer onwards

Outdoors
Sowing time (inside) mid-spring
Planting-out time early summer
Planting distance (cordon) 45cm/18in
Planting distance (bush) 60cm/24in
Distance between sown rows 75cm/30in
Harvesting late summer onwards

PESTS AND DISEASES

Tomato plants suffer from a number of pests and diseases. Fortunately, these are generally not troublesome enough to deter those who grow them. Pests include aphids, potato cyst eelworm, whitefly and red spider mite. Diseases include tomato blight, grey mould, potato mosaic virus, greenback, tomato leaf mould and scald. Many problems can be avoided by good ventilation, but you will need to consult a specialist if you have persistent problems. Cracked or split fruit are often the result of uneven watering, the last excessive watering being the final culprit. Watering regularly should avoid this.

GROWING TOMATOES

Using grow bags
Tomatoes can be grown in bags of compost (soil mix). Simply remove the marked sections and plant directly into the bag. The plastic bag helps to reduce water loss in hot weather.

Pinching out the side shoots
The side shoots on cordon varieties should be pinched or cut out when they appear. This helps to direct the plant's energy into its fruit rather than its leaf.

Harvesting the fruit
The colour of the tomato when ripe will depend on the variety. However, if the fruit comes away from the stem easily it is ready to be eaten.

Ripening green tomatoes
If the weather has been poor, and many tomatoes have failed to ripen on the plant, dig up any remaining plants and hang them upside down under protection. This may be in the kitchen or in a greenhouse or garage. They will ripen slowly and will often keep until mid-winter if treated in this way.

Hanging basket tomatoes
A few varieties are suitable for hanging baskets, and can even be grown with ornamental plants, but they will need very frequent watering and feeding.

Guide to Buying Tomatoes

Nowadays, there is a wider choice of tomatoes available than ever before, and they vary in colour, shape and size as well as flavour.

In the past, the range of tomatoes sold in supermarkets was fairly limited, and if you wanted to try different varieties the only option was to grow your own. The market has now changed, and supermarkets recognize the consumers' distaste for tomatoes that have been picked too young, ripened artificially and as a consequence are bland and watery.

As a result, many more varieties of tomato are now on sale, and supermarkets commission growers to breed tomatoes that fit their requirements exactly: from sweetness and colour to skin thickness and shape. All these factors can be varied by careful cross-pollination and generations of selective breeding.

This has led to a situation unusual in the vegetable and fruit world, namely that the tomato is one of a few vegetables that have been branded. When a supermarket chain commissions a grower to breed a tomato exclusively for sale in their stores, a new "own-brand" name is chosen, which does not reveal the tomato's origins, even though it might be a hybrid of a familiar variety.

Fortunately, when shopping for tomatoes, we tend to be concerned with flavour, texture or shape and are not too worried about the name. Apart from these basic characteristics, ripeness and freshness most affect the quality. The best tomatoes are usually found at a local market, particularly those run by farmers themselves. The tomatoes will have been allowed to ripen longer than most and picked just before they are transported to the market.

When purchasing tomatoes, also look for those that have been organically grown. These tomatoes will have been cultivated using sustainable farming practices and without the use of pesticides and synthetic fertilizers. They have a naturally lower water content and so usually have a better flavour and texture than most. Whichever variety you choose, be adventurous and try something new.

Beefsteak tomatoes

These are pumpkin-shaped, large and sometimes ridged. They are usually deep red or orange in colour. They have a good firm texture, plenty of flesh, and a sweet, mellow flavour due to their low acidity and often high water content. They are best eaten raw in salads and sandwiches or stuffed and baked whole.

Round or salad tomatoes

The round or salad tomato is the most common type available, they vary in size according to the exact variety and the time of year. Their flavour varies considerably depending on whether they are grown and picked during their natural season. They are generally quite acidic with a full flavour, so are excellent for cooking or eating raw. For cooking, look for fruit that is soft and very red. Add a pinch of sugar to bring out the sweetness and season well with salt and pepper to bring out the flavour.

Cherry tomatoes

These small, dainty cherry-size tomatoes are mouthwateringly sweet. High in sugar and low in acid, they are good in salads or for cooking whole. The skin can be very delicate in summer months, but tends to toughen towards the end of the season. They are perfect as part of a cocktail snack as they are just the right size for one mouthful. Combine them with cheese on sticks, or if you have time, make them into a brightly coloured hors d'oeuvres by stuffing them with soft cheese mixed with red or green pesto. They were once prized treasures exclusive to gardeners but are now widely available in supermarkets. Although they are more expensive than the usual round or salad tomatoes, it's worth paying a little extra for the delicious flavour which, remarkably, improves even further with keeping. Red, yellow and orange varieties of cherry tomato are available.

Plum tomatoes

These tomatoes are elongated and are usually shaped like an egg, but are occasionally very long and almost hollow inside. They have a meaty flesh, a thick core, strong skin, which can be easily peeled, and are richly flavoured, with fewer seeds than round tomatoes. They are considered to be the best cooking tomatoes due to their concentrated flavour and high acidity. They are best used when they are fully ripe. Plum tomatoes are grown widely in Italy, and are available in various sizes and colours, but red plum tomatoes are best for cooking. They are the most popular variety for canning.

Guide to Buying Tomatoes

Yellow tomatoes

These have a sweet, slightly lemony, mild flavour and a lower acidity than red tomatoes. Yellow tomatoes come in different shapes and sizes, from pear, to plum and round. Yellow tomatoes should ideally be used in salads and also for garnishes for their decorative quality, but are quite suitable for cooking and are especially good in pickles and chutneys. The Yellow Pear variety, so called because of the shape, is particularly popular.

Orange tomatoes

Mild tomatoes, these have a sweet, delicate flavour and low acidity. Like red, round salad tomatoes, they have quite a high seed to flesh ratio. The seeds, however, are often smaller than in the red tomato. Orange tomatoes add a splash of colour to salads, create wonderful garnishes and are also good in soups. They make stunning sauces. Orange Bourgoin and Mini Orange are particularly pretty varieties.

Green tomatoes

The term "green tomato" was used for the tangy, unripened tomatoes traditionally used for relishes and chutneys. Ripe green tomatoes are also available now – such as the green cherry tomato "Green Grape", and the cordons "Evergreen" and stripy "Green Zebra". They have a bright green skin and flesh, and are tasty and very decorative used in salads and garnishes.

Vine tomatoes

These tomatoes were recently introduced in supermarkets, and were greeted with great enthusiasm. The tomatoes are just the same as other tomatoes, but are still attached to their stalk or vine and have the aromatic quality usually only present in home-grown tomatoes. This is mostly due to the chemicals coming from the green stalk and leaf of the plant, rather than the fruit itself. However, if you do not have home-grown tomatoes, choose rich red vine tomatoes over round, salad tomatoes.

Pear tomatoes

This small category includes some of the tastiest tomatoes of all. The name refers to the shape, not the flavour, and the tomatoes are generally quite small. Perhaps the best known is the Yellow Pear, a vigorous grower that produces masses of tiny yellow fruits. They look pretty on the plate, and have a mild, citrus flavour. Red Pear tomatoes have a richer flavour and are equally popular. In tomato tastings, these score very highly for flavour.

SELECTING TOMATOES

Tomatoes are at their best when they have ripened naturally in the sun – they should ideally be allowed to ripen slowly on the plant so that their flavour can fully develop. Therefore, home-grown tomatoes are best for flavour, followed by those grown and sold locally. Try to buy tomatoes loose so that you can smell them before you buy – they should have a wonderful aroma, not only from the green stalks, but also from the tomato itself. When buying tomatoes from a supermarket or greengrocer, look at the leafy green tops: the fresher they look the better. If you are buying red tomatoes, try to buy deep-red fruit. If buying yellow or orange, look for depth of colour. The fruit should have flesh that is firm, but gives slightly when pressed gently. Choose tomatoes according to how you wish to prepare them – buy locally grown beefsteak or cherry tomatoes for salads, and plum tomatoes for sauces.

STORING TOMATOES

If you are not using the tomatoes the same day, they will benefit from being removed from the packaging. To improve the flavour of a slightly hard tomato, leave it to ripen at room temperature and preferably in direct sunlight. Paler tomatoes or those tinged with green will redden if kept in a brown paper bag or fruit bowl with a ripe tomato or banana; the gases given off will ripen the tomatoes, though they cannot improve the basic flavour. Overripe tomatoes, where the skin has split and they seem to be bursting with juice, are excellent in soups and sauces. However, check for any sign of mould or decay, as this would spoil the flavour of the finished product. Tomatoes should not be stored in the refrigerator – chilling adversely affects the taste and the texture, so aim to make small, frequent purchases to enjoy them at their best.

Useful Equipment

The right tool for the job always makes life easier, and you may find that there are now pieces of equipment available that you haven't come across before. Although it is perfectly possible to use only basic kitchen tools for tomatoes, this list will help you to make the most of what is available.

FOOD PROCESSOR OR BLENDER

An invaluable asset when preparing tomatoes is a food processor. Use the main chopping blade to finely chop peeled or unpeeled tomatoes for recipes where the texture of the tomato or finished product is important. A food processor is perfect for dishes such as soups, stews and chunky salsas.

Below: A blender is perfect for quickly making a smooth tomato sauce.

MOULI GRATER

Use a mouli grater to produce a smooth tomato purée (paste) – the consistency will depend upon the ripeness of the tomatoes. Very ripe tomatoes will give a more liquid result, while firmer tomatoes will produce a thicker purée. Tomatoes can be cooked with other vegetables such as (bell) peppers or courgettes (zucchini) and then processed in the mouli to make tasty purées for babies.

KNIVES AND KNIFE SHARPENERS

You will need several types of knives to prepare tomatoes, and it is important that the appropriate knife should be used for each job – for efficiency and safety reasons. To slice tomatoes, the best knife is a small serrated one, which is easy to control and can be used to produce thick or thin slices according to preference. For smaller, awkward jobs, such as peeling or seeding tomatoes, a paring knife is ideal. Choose a knife with a short enough blade to allow you to use your thumb as well, but not too

Below: The knife on the left is a special tomato knife, the others are paring knives.

Below: A mouli grater is handy for puréeing small quantities of food.

short or the balance will be less than ideal. For jobs other than slicing, the knife blade should be curved with a sharp point. Don't be tempted by those with removable peeler blades, as these are easily lost and remove too much skin. One of the handiest knives has a wide, serrated blade that ends in a round, flat surface for lifting the slice on to a sandwich or salad. It is now usually made of stainless steel with a wooden handle. This was designed in 1920, has recently been brought back into production by various companies and is available for purchase again. However, if you are lucky enough, you may find an original 1920s version.

Useful Equipment 15

Knives must always be sharp and clean – a blunt knife is more likely to cause injury because excessive pressure has to be used. If you can't cut the skin of a tomato with a knife, the blade needs sharpening. There are several types of knife sharpener available, ranging from a traditional steel or carborundum, which gives the best results but can be quite tricky to use, to manual or electrical sharpeners, which will give a good edge. Whichever type of sharpener you use, make sure you sharpen your knives regularly and evenly – uneven sharpening can be dangerous. Knives will stay sharper if they are used on a cutting board.

Right: Peelers are useful when making garnishes.

SWIVEL-BLADE VEGETABLE PEELER

With their horizontal-angled blades, these easy-to-use peelers are ideal for peeling fine swirls of tomato skin to make garnishes such as tomato roses.

TOMATO PRESS

A tomato press is a useful piece of equipment for dealing with a glut of tomatoes. It looks rather like a modern version of an old-fashioned mincer or grinder, and clips to the work surface. Put the tomatoes in the bowl at the top, turn a handle, and smooth tomato pulp comes out of one side, while seeds and skin emerge from the other.

CRINKLE CUTTER

This is a specially designed knife, which has a crinkle-edged blade to give a decorative wavy edge to fruits and vegetables. It can be used to cut tomatoes in halves, quarters or slices for attractive garnishes.

Above: Sieves are handy for making smooth soups and sauces.

SIEVE

A sturdy sieve can be used to produce smooth purées (pastes), sauces and soups. A metal sieve is preferable to a plastic one because it can withstand higher temperatures and enables you to sieve hot and cold mixtures; it is also easier to keep clean. Conical sieves have the advantage of forcing the tomato sauce, soup or purée mixture out through a smaller surface area so there is less risk of splashing and the sieved food can be passed into a smaller container. To sieve tomato mixtures, the best method is to push down firmly using the back of a metal or wooden spoon – this ensures minimum wastage and maximum yield. It is best if the tomatoes have been skinned if this method is used.

HULLING TOOL

This is a handy little implement used to remove the stalk and green part from the top of individual tomatoes while leaving the fruit intact. It is especially useful and can save time, if you are preparing a large glut of home-grown tomatoes to make into sauces and soups for the freezer.

JUICER

There are principally two types of juicer on the market: mechanical and electrical. The electrical ones suit tomatoes best as they will separate out the skin and fibre, leaving a thick and delicious drink in moments. When buying a juicer, the best type for tomatoes is a centrifugal juicer – the tomatoes simply need to be cut into pieces (there is no need to peel or seed) and then put into the feeder. If you wish to experiment and make fruit and vegetable cocktails, you may need to check whether the juicer will process harder ingredients, such as carrots and celery, too.

Above: A juicer is great for making fresh, healthy tomato drinks.

Preparing Tomatoes

For perfect results, use the following techniques to prepare tomatoes and make attractive garnishes.

PEELING

Add a professional finish to sauces and soups that are not being sieved by peeling and seeding the tomatoes.

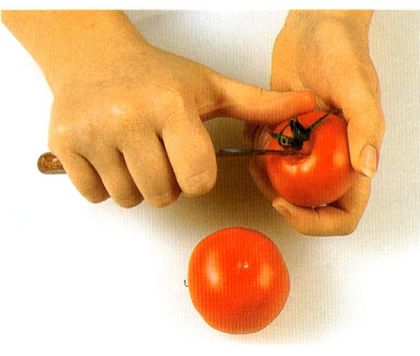

1 Use a small, sharp knife to cut out the green stalk end, then make a cross in the skin on the base of each tomato.

2 Place the tomatoes in a bowl and add boiling water to cover. Leave for 30 seconds, then drain. Cool slightly.

3 Gently pull away the loosened skin from the tomato.

FLAME-SKINNING

If you have a gas stove, this is the simplest and quickest method for skinning a small number of tomatoes. If you have many more than five or six tomatoes, then the first method is quicker.

1 Skewer one tomato at a time on a metal fork or skewer and hold in a gas flame for 1–2 minutes, turning the tomato until the skin splits and wrinkles.

2 Use a cloth to protect your hands and remove the tomato from the fork or skewer. Leave the tomatoes on a chopping board until cool enough to handle. Using your fingers or a knife, slip off and discard the skins.

PLAIN CUTTING

Tomato slices have a different appearance, depending on which way you cut them. Slice them across rather than downwards for salads and pizzas – the slices have a more attractive finish this way, and hold the seeds in the flesh better. For wedges, cut the tomato downwards, then quarter. If smaller pieces are needed, cut the quarters into two or three pieces, depending on the size of the tomato.

SEEDING

Using just the flesh of the tomato gives a meatier texture to a dish. Here are two methods that can be used.

Halve the tomatoes. Squeeze out the seeds or scoop them out with a teaspoon.

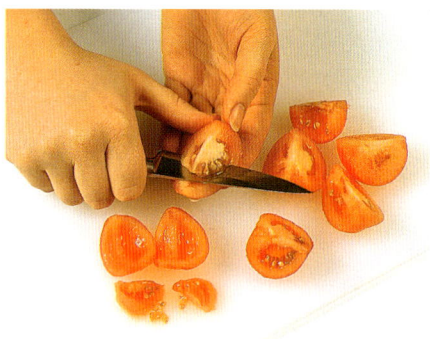

Cut the tomatoes into quarters. Slide a knife along the inner flesh, scooping out all the seeds.

CONCASSING

After peeling and seeding tomatoes, to add the final touch to the perfect sauce or soup ingredient, concass the flesh.

Using a sharp knife, cut the flesh into neat 5mm/¼in squares.

Preparing Tomatoes 17

TOMATO ROSES

Use these classic tomato roses to decorate quiches or tarts or to garnish platters of cold meats.

1 Use a swivel-blade peeler to peel one long continuous strip from a whole tomato. Start at the base and work slowly to avoid breaking the strip.

2 With the skin side out, and starting at the stem end, coil the peel loosely to within 2cm/¾in of the end. Set the coil upright so that it resembles a rosebud and tuck the end loosely underneath.

3 Place a lettuce leaf underneath the rose to give a contrast and to add the finishing touch.

TOMATO SUNS

These pretty cherry tomato garnishes can be arranged on individual plates for a professional looking garnish.

1 Hull a cherry tomato, then place it stem-side down. Cut lightly into the skin across the top, edging the knife towards the base. Turn the tomato through 45° and repeat, until the skin has been cut into eight segments, joined at the base.

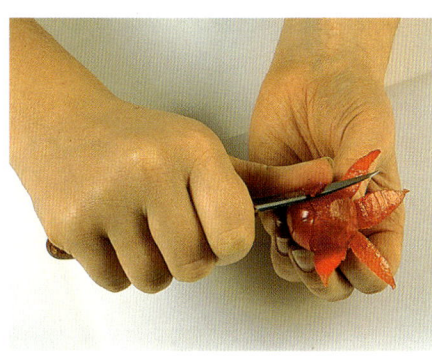

2 Slide the knife under the point of each segment and ease the skin away, stopping just short of the base.

3 With your fingers or the knife, gently fold the "petals" on each tomato back to mimic the sun's rays.

TOMATO FANS

This simply prepared garnish can transform a plain pâté or dip. It looks good next to a sandwich, too.

1 Quarter and seed a tomato. Make four cuts down most of the length of each piece. Fan out the "fingers".

2 Top each tomato fan with a sprig of parsley, to finish.

TOMATO LILIES

Using a small sharp knife, make identical zig-zag cuts around the central circumference. Cut right into the centre of the tomato. Gently pull the halves apart and top with cucumber.

Preserving Tomatoes

If you've got a glut of tomatoes or simply can't resist the bargain-priced tomatoes at the market, there are plenty of ways to keep your supply going right through the winter.

BOTTLED CHERRY TOMATOES

Cherry tomatoes bottled in their own juices with garlic and basil are sweetly delicious and a perfect accompaniment to thick slices of country ham.

MAKES 1KG/2¼LB

INGREDIENTS
- 1kg/2¼lb cherry tomatoes
- 5ml/1 tsp salt per 1 litre/1¾ pint/ 4 cup jar
- 5ml/1 tsp granulated sugar per 1 litre/1¾ pint/4 cup jar
- fresh basil leaves
- 5 garlic cloves per jar

1 Preheat the oven to 120°C/250°F/Gas ½. Prick each tomato with a fork. Pack them into clean, dry jars, adding the salt and sugar as you go.

2 Fill the jars to within 2cm/¾in of the top. Tuck the basil and garlic among the tomatoes. Rest the lids on the jars, but do not seal. Stand the jars on a baking sheet lined with a layer of newspaper and place in the oven. After about 45 minutes, when the juice is simmering, remove the jars from the oven and seal. Store in a cool place and use within 6 months.

DRYING AND PRESERVING IN OIL

Dried tomatoes have always been popular with the Italians – it's a wonderful way to enjoy the taste of summer in the winter months. To make your own dried tomatoes by "oven drying" them,

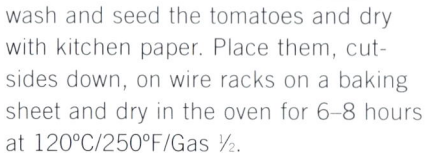

wash and seed the tomatoes and dry with kitchen paper. Place them, cut-sides down, on wire racks on a baking sheet and dry in the oven for 6–8 hours at 120°C/250°F/Gas ½.

Home-dried tomatoes can be preserved in olive oil for up to 6 months. Simply place them in clean jars and top up with olive oil. The tomatoes will taste truly delicious and the oil will take on a wonderful tomato flavour which is delicious used in salad dressings.

FREEZING

Whole, fresh tomatoes do not freeze well, as they tend to go mushy once thawed. However, if you have a glut of tomatoes, they freeze very well once they have been puréed: skin and core the tomatoes, boil with minimal water for 5 minutes, then purée in a food processor. Allow to cool and then freeze. The pureé (paste) can be added to stews, soups and casseroles.

TOMATO KETCHUP

The real tomato flavour of this home-made ketchup is delicious with burgers.

MAKES 2.75KG/6LB

INGREDIENTS
- 2.25kg/5lb very ripe tomatoes
- 1 celery heart, chopped
- 30ml/2 tbsp soft light brown sugar
- 65ml/4½ tbsp raspberry vinegar
- 3 garlic cloves
- 15ml/1 tbsp salt
- 1 onion
- 6 cloves
- 4 allspice berries
- 6 black peppercorns
- 1 rosemary sprig
- 25g/1oz fresh root ginger, sliced

1 Peel, seed and cut the tomatoes into small pieces, then place them in a large pan with the celery, sugar, vinegar, garlic and salt. Tie the onion, rosemary and spices in a double layer of muslin (cheesecloth) and add to the pan.

2 Bring the mixture to the boil, then simmer for 2 hours, stirring regularly to ensure the mixture does not stick to the base of the pan. Cook until the mixture is reduced by half. Remove the cloth bag containing the onion, rosemary and spices.

3 Purée the mixture in a blender or sieve, then return to the pan and simmer for 15 minutes. Bottle in clean, sterilized glass jars with a good seal. Store in the refrigerator and use within 2 weeks.

Left and above: Bottled tomatoes and ketchup are delicious and easy to make.

Tomatoes in the Pantry

When fresh tomatoes are out of season or unavailable, or because it is more convenient, you'll be able to get a distinctive tomato flavour in seconds, simply by opening a jar, can or bottle. The following guide will help you to choose the most appropriate product for your recipe.

CANNED TOMATOES

Tomatoes are one of the few fruits that can be canned really successfully and they are the most popular tomato pantry product available. They are excellent in tomato sauces for pastas and pizzas, having an intense and distinct flavour, and can be puréed when passata is called for. Plum tomatoes are normally selected for canning and can be whole or chopped. Flavoured canned tomatoes are also available. These have added herbs or garlic, but it is preferable to avoid these as the flavours can be overwhelming. It is better to add your own flavourings.

PASSATA

Raw, ripe tomatoes that have been puréed and sieved to remove the skin and seeds are known and packaged as passata. Depending on the degree of sieving, it can be perfectly smooth or slightly chunky. The chunky variety is sold in tall jars, while the smoothest type is available in jars or cartons. It may separate, if it has been standing for some time, but will mix together again if it is shaken a few times. It is a useful pantry ingredient and is invaluable in recipes such as soups where you want a smooth finished result in minutes. With the addition of just a little salt and a few herbs, it makes an almost instant sauce for pasta dishes.

SUGOCASA

This is a combination of coarsely chopped plum tomatoes and tomato purée (paste). It has a rich, full flavour and is more concentrated than passata. Sold in jars, sugocasa is ideal for pizzas, pasta sauces and stews.

RED PESTO

Pesto, a traditional Italian ingredient, is usually made with basil, pine nuts, Parmesan or Pecorino cheese and olive oil. A red version of pesto is available that has either sun-dried tomatoes or red (bell) peppers added. The overwhelming flavour is of basil, with the tomato or pepper being added for colour and just a hint of flavour.

CREAMED TOMATOES

These are usually sold in cardboard and plastic cartons of varying sizes. They have a very smooth and thick consistency and often contain many preservatives. However, they are very convenient as you can buy a carton smaller than a can, which is the perfect quantity for a soup or sauce if you are cooking for just one or two people.

SUN-DRIED TOMATOES

These wonderfully rich tomatoes, which are actually more often air-dried by machine rather than by the sun, have an intense, sweet flavour. They are available either dried and sold in packets or preserved in olive oil in jars. The packet variety can be either eaten on their own as a snack or rehydrated in hot water until soft for cooking (use the tomato-flavoured water for soups or sauces). Sun-dried tomatoes preserved in oil can simply be drained and chopped and added straight to a dish or eaten as they are. The oil in which they are preserved takes on a wonderful tomato flavour and can be used for cooking or to make a fabulous salad dressing. Use these tasty preserved tomatoes in soups, pasta sauces or as an Italian-style appetizer, served with mozzarella, fresh tomatoes and basil.

TOMATO PURÉE

Available in cans or in tubes, tomato purée (paste) adds a strong flavour and a very bright colour to sauces and soups. It should be used very sparingly because the flavour is quite intense and could overpower the flavour of other ingredients. Sun-dried tomato paste is also available and has the rich taste of the dried tomatoes. It is even more concentrated than regular purée, because the tomatoes have been dried and preserved in oil. You may wish to reduce the amount of oil in a recipe if you are going to use this type of purée. Tomato purée should be stored in the refrigerator once opened – tubes will keep for up to 6 months and cans of purée can be kept for up to 1 week.

The Tastier Tomato

A well-flavoured tomato needs little enhancement, but there are a number of herbs and spices that complement and enliven the flavour of tomato dishes particularly well.

GARLIC
Allium sativum

Intensely fragrant and pungent, garlic has an affinity with tomatoes in numerous dishes, both hot and cold. Like onions, garlic is much milder in flavour when cooked, and can be crushed, sliced or chopped. Cloves are delicious roasted whole with tomatoes and extra virgin olive oil.

CHIVES
Allium schoenoprasum

These familiar long, thin, tubular green leaves have a mild, onion-like flavour. Chinese, Welsh or garlic chives are also mild, but have a hint of garlic in their flavour. Snip into small pieces with scissors and add to tomato salads, dressings, dips, omelettes and soups, and use as a garnish. Chives look pretty when braided, tied in a bow, or simply placed on the side of a dish.

PAPRIKA
Capsicum annuum

This rich, bright red powder is derived from a pepper that looks very like the sweet red (bell) pepper. It is widely grown in Europe, especially Hungary, and the USA. It works well with tomatoes and is the principal flavouring in goulash. Look out for pimentón dulce, which is a delicious smoked paprika from Spain.

CHILLIES
Capsicum annuum

These are actually from the same family as the tomato, so they have a natural affinity. You'll find the hot spice of chilli and sweetness of tomatoes combined in many traditional Mexican and South American dishes. The heat varies, depending on variety, but generally the smaller the chilli, the hotter it is. For a milder flavour, discard the seeds.

CINNAMON
Cinnamomum zeylanicum

The fragrant bark of a tree that is native to Sri Lanka, cinnamon is used in both sweet and savoury dishes. Its warm flavour goes well with tomatoes and chillies, a combination that often appears in Moroccan and Greek cooking. Use sticks whole, or grind fresh for the finest flavour.

CORIANDER (CILANTRO)
Coriandrum sativum

Delicate green leaves with a strong, warm, earthy flavour. Use generously in raw tomato dishes, or add towards the end of cooking to retain the flavour. Good with chilli spiced dishes.

BAY
Laurus nobilis

The slightly sweet, astringent, spicy flavour of bay is ideal for infusing into long-cooked tomato dishes such as sauces or stews, as the flavour increases with cooking. Tie the leaves into bunches and remove them before serving. Dried bay leaves are less bitter in flavour than fresh.

MINT
Mentha spicata

Fresh green leaves with a clean, refreshing flavour, favoured by the ancient Romans. Spearmint or garden mint is the main variety, though there are many other types, such as applemint and peppermint. Use it to enliven tomato soups, relishes, dips or salads. For a delicious but unusual sandwich filling, try combining sweet red tomatoes and home-produced mint jelly.

NUTMEG AND MACE
Myristica fragrans

Both have a sweet, warm, rich flavour that adds a subtle depth to tomato sauces, soups and pasta dishes. Nutmeg is sometimes used in Greek moussaka. Use nutmeg freshly grated for the best, most fragrant flavour.

BASIL
Ocimum basilicum

Tomatoes and basil are classic partners, particularly in Italian dishes. Basil has a strong, aromatic and peppery flavour. Tear the fresh leaves over a tomato salad, or use basil oil for a dressing. To keep the aromatic quality, it is best added to hot dishes at the very end of cooking.

MARJORAM
Origanum majorana

A delicate, soft-leaved herb with a sweet, spicy, fragrant flavour. It is very good in egg-based tomato dishes, or when added to the filling for stuffed tomatoes and mild-flavoured vegetarian dishes.

OREGANO
Origanum vulgare

This is a form of wild marjoram, with a strong fragrant flavour similar to cultivated marjoram. It is widely used in Greek and Italian dishes, and is particularly good with tomatoes in fish dishes, in tomato sauces and on pizzas and sprinkled on to salads.

PARSLEY
Petroselinum crispum

Both flat leaved and curly varieties are used in cooking, but the flat leaved variety is superior in flavour and is more tender to eat. It is often used with tomatoes in classic dishes such as Middle-eastern Tabbouleh and along with coriander (cilantro), it often appears in Mexican salsa recipes.

PEPPERCORNS
Piper nigrum

Dried berries from a vine that originated in the East Indies, peppercorns are commonplace today, but were once treated like treasure. Used whole or ground, they add a warm spiciness to ketchup and other tomato sauces.

ROSEMARY
Rosmarinus officinalis

These aromatic, pungent, resinous leaves go well with tomatoes in cooked meat dishes or in marinades, or can be used as a garnish. They can be used finely chopped or in sprigs to remove after cooking.

SAGE
Salvia officinalis

Silver green sage and tomatoes are old friends. An early English cookbook recommended strewing sage over tomatoes before baking, and young leaves also taste good in a tomato salad, or snipped into the filling for a stuffed tomato.

WINTER SAVORY
Saturea montana

Both winter and summer savory (*Saturea hortensis*) have a pungent, slightly peppery flavour that adds interest to tomato sauces, soups and drinks based upon tomato juice. It is a little-used herb, but really does taste wonderfully savoury with tomatoes. Use fresh or dried.

THYME
Thymus vulgaris

The scent of thyme is so sweet that it is sometimes planted on paths, so that when the leaves are crushed they will perfume the air. There are several types, the most common being a shrubby plant with a very pungent flavour. It is most often cultivated, but can occasionally be found wild. It goes well with tomatoes, aubergines (eggplant), courgettes (zucchini) and onions, so is often added to ratatouille.

Above: Tomatoes and fresh herbs are a match made in heaven.

Guide to Tomato Varieties

There are more than 7,000 varieties of tomato, with new hybrids coming on line all the time. In choosing which types to feature in this round-up, flavour was the first priority, but second was to give some idea of how varied this versatile ingredient can be. Tomatoes come in a range of sizes, from dwarf varieties, scarcely bigger than a grape, to heavies that weigh in at more than 1.3kg/3lb. They can be round, plum, or pear shaped; squat, smooth or ribbed, and their looks can even mimic (bell) peppers. Colours range from palest cream to dark purple, and there are striped varieties that particularly appeal to children. Some are perfect for snacks and salads, others are best cooked, but all are well worth getting to know. For the finest, freshest flavour, grow them yourself, or buy them from someone who shares your enthusiasm and grows several different varieties. Farmer's markets and organic growers are good sources. The tomatoes you see in the supermarket are often specific to that chain of stores, which is why the names may not be as familiar as those you grow at home.

AILSA CRAIG

This tomato was bred by a Scottish grower in Ayrshire, and takes its name from a rocky island in the Firth of Clyde. It is grown both outdoors and under glass. The mid-red fruits are medium-size, about 5cm/2in in diameter, with smooth, thick skin. Ailsa Craig has good sweet flavour. It is the source of several successful hybrids.

Right: Ailsa Craig

Below: Alicante

ALICANTE

An early maturing English cordon-type tomato, Alicante is regarded as a good choice for novice gardeners, as it is not difficult to grow, and crops very well. The medium-size fruits are uniform, smooth and red, with a very good flavour. Alicante tomatoes remain firm when grilled (broiled), roasted or baked, and are ideal for mixed vegetable kebabs.

Below: Ararat Flamed

ARARAT FLAMED

Bred from a Hungarian variety, Debrecen, this good-looking tomato is clearly flamed, with dark green stripes on the skin, which fade as the fruit ripens. It is a cordon type, with a big yield and good flavour.

> **Hybrid tomatoes**
>
> These are scientifically bred from at least two parent tomatoes, which possess desirable characteristics such as disease resistance or colour, with the aim of producing a tomato that combines both features.

BRANDYWINE

The original Brandywine was developed in America by Amish farmers in the latter half of the 19th century. The plants yield well and are disease-resistant, making them a popular choice with gardeners and growers alike. The vines grow quite tall, and have leaves that resemble those of potatoes. The reddish-pink fruits – up to 900g/2lb in weight – are noted for their succulent, rich flavour. The good balance of sweetness and acidity makes this tomato a top choice for salads.

Below: Brandywine

BRITAIN'S BREAKFAST

Thick-skinned, with a superb flavour, this tomato is shaped like a lemon and is about the size of a small hen's egg. It has a striking growth pattern, with very large spreading trusses, each capable of producing more than 60 fruits. Britain's Breakfast has a sweet taste and is good raw or cooked.

Above: Britain's Breakfast

Guide to Tomato Varieties 23

CHADWICK

This bright red cherry tomato is named in honour of Alan Chadwick, who developed the biointensive method of gardening. The vigorous, disease-resistant plants bear extremely well. Chadwick tomatoes measure about 2.5cm/1in across, and grow in clusters of five or six. They have a tangy flavour and taste good raw in salads or cooked in soups or sauces.

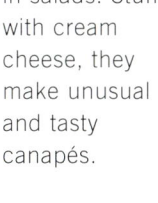

Above: Chadwick

DAFFODEL

These canary yellow tomatoes were bred in Britain, and are based on Gardener's Delight, a popular cordon type. Tasty and sweet, they are perfect for lunch boxes, or can be incorporated in salads. Stuffed with cream cheese, they make unusual and tasty canapés.

Above: Daffodel

Below: Dark Purple Beefsteak

DARK PURPLE BEEFSTEAK

There are a number of varieties of beefsteak tomato, all big on flavour as well as size. Some specimens are so large that a single slice can be sufficient to fill a roll or sandwich. These tomatoes are also good for stuffing. The solid, meaty flesh is full of old-fashioned tomato flavour. The classic beefsteak (or beef) tomato is red, but specialities such as this dark purple variety (more often deep pink) and the pale rose Florida Pink are becoming increasingly popular. Most weigh between 350g/12oz and 450g/1lb, but there are also giant varieties including the aptly named Goliath, which can top 1.3kg/3lb. For flavour, Aunt Ginny's Purple and Big Beef are consistent favourites.

FLAMME

This French cordon-type tomato is an excellent cropper. The spherical fruits, about the size of golf balls, are a beautiful apricot-orange colour and look pretty when cut. The flesh is juicy, with an intense fruity flavour, making this tomato an excellent choice for salads and salsas. Flamme also makes a good pasta sauce, and can be dried successfully.

Right: Flamme

GARDENER'S DELIGHT

One of the older varieties of British tomato, this is perennially popular. It is easy to grow, both outdoors and in the greenhouse, and yields a heavy crop. Long trusses bear clusters of dark red fruits, about 4cm/1½in in diameter. This variety has a slight tendency to split, but the flesh is meaty, with a sweet yet tangy flavour that connoisseurs claim is what tomatoes used to taste like in the days before they were bred to meet commercial rather than culinary criteria.

Left: Gardener's Delight

Left: Golden Sunrise

GOLDEN SUNRISE

This cordon type is a heavy, reliable cropper, producing masses of medium-size round fruit. As the name suggests, these are sunshine yellow in colour. The flavour is sweet and fruity, with a slight suggestion of citrus. Slices look pretty in a two-tomato salad, and these tomatoes make an excellent garnish. Try them diced, with a light vinaigrette and a dusting of chopped mint.

Left: Green Zebra

GREEN ZEBRA

As you would expect from the name, this one has stripes (dark green on a yellowish-green background, which strengthen with ripening) and looks very attractive. The tomatoes are about 7.5cm/3in across and weigh around 75g/3oz apiece. Cut them to reveal emerald green flesh with an exquisitely sweet/spicy flavour and a subtle tang. Children love them, so put them into lunch boxes or serve in salads.

HARBINGER

This English cordon-type tomato was first bred around the beginning of the 20th century. It can be grown outdoors and under glass. It is indeed a harbinger of summer, and fruits early, producing medium-size tomatoes with thin, smooth skins. Harbingers have a balanced, old-fashioned tomato flavour. The fruits ripen rapidly, both on the plant and after picking. They are good tomatoes for salads and garnishes.

Above: Harbinger

JUBILEE

An American variety of tomato that requires staking, this yields medium to large globe-shaped fruits that are a rich golden yellow or orange colour. The flavour is mild and low in acidity. Alternate slices of Jubilee and Alicante look pretty on a tomato Tarte Tatin, or make the most of their colour by combining them with shellfish and pasta in a creamy saffron sauce.

Below: Jubilee

Below: Koenig Humbert

KOENIG HUMBERT

Named in honour of Italy's King Umberto, this is a very old medium-early variety. It was popular in North America in the early part of the 20th century. After 1920 it became somewhat less fashionable, but as an heirloom or heritage variety it is now making a comeback. The bright scarlet 50g/2oz fruits can be prune- or pear-shaped, and are very juicy and sweet.

Below: Lycopersicon Ribesforme

LYCOPERSICON RIBESFORME

Despite the gravitas of its botanical name, this is a small fruit. It is a short-lived perennial that was bred from the wild cherry tomato, and has a semi-erect, scrambling habit. As with many of the smaller tomatoes, the ratio of skin to flesh is high, so these are best grown under glass for a more tender skin. Otherwise, if the trusses are picked whole, they make a magnificent table decoration and are ideal for garnishing.

MARMANDE

One of the few types of tomato that most people know by name, Marmande originated in Provence. It does particularly well in Mediterranean regions, but will also grow in cooler climes. Aromatic and fruity, these ribbed tomatoes are good for cooking and are frequently stuffed. They are best grown outdoors, as they need bees for pollination.

Above: Marmande

MINI ORANGE

Quite popular a few years ago, but now less frequently grown, this is a bush variety that produces masses of small (2.5–4cm/1–1½in) round fruits. It is particularly notable for its brilliant orange colour. This is a rewarding variety to grow.

Above: Mini Orange

Right: Mirabelle

MIRABELLE

Similar to Gardener's Delight in all but size and colour, this has small yellow fruits with a sweet flavour. Plants of medium height produce long, heavily laden trusses. Mirabelle tomatoes make a pretty garnish and are good in salsas and salads. If you are fortunate enough to have a heavy crop, they make a delicous chutney.

Below: Moon Beam

MOON BEAM

This early-ripening tomato is a beefsteak type. Unlike many beefsteaks, which tend to be squat, the glossy orange fruits are almost spherical. Slices taste good in sandwiches and hamburgers, and the tomatoes can also be used to make a very tasty tomato jam.

ORANGE BOURGOIN

About the same size as apricots, and almost the same colour, these juicy tomatoes have a superb flavour. Fruity, mild and sweet, they are perfect for nibbling, and taste delicious in a salad with sweet orange (bell) peppers and bright segments of orange on rocket (arugula) leaves.

Above: Orange Bourgoin

PENDULINA

This is a prolific, tumbling variety of cherry tomato, often grown in hanging baskets or tubs. The fruits are bite size, and have a distinctive pointed tip. They may be yellow, orange or red, and have sweet, juicy flesh.

Right: Pendulina Yellow

Try something new

It is tempting to grow the same tomatoes every year, especially when you are on to a winner such as Gardener's Delight, but do try some of the new varieties (or newly available heirlooms) as well.

Guide to Tomato Varieties 25

26 Guide to Tomato Varieties

Right: Peruvian Horn

PERUVIAN HORN

Also known as Andine Cornue, this variety was recently introduced by a collector who brought it back from the Andes. The fruits are very large and look rather like poblano chillies or sweet (bell) peppers with pointed ends. They are particularly good for cooking, and make fine soups and sauces.

Below: Phydra

PHYDRA

Perfect for growing in hanging baskets or tubs, this 30cm/12in-high plant produces cascades of very small fruits in various colours. Children love them for their appearance and sweet flavour, and they also look very good as a garnish, especially when left on the vine.

PINK PING PONG

A robust variety, this ripens early and produces masses of unusual pinkish-red fruits the size of ping pong balls. The fruits are juicy, with a very good, sweet flavour, perfect for eating in the hand, or adding to salads.

Above: Pink Ping Pong

PRINCIPE BORGHESE

Although largely identified as a paste tomato, this aromatic Italian bush variety tastes good raw, and can also be dried very successfully. The ovoid, medium-size fruits (about 50g/2oz) are carried on large trusses and are very sugary. When grown in cooler climes, the flavour is refreshing, slightly more acidic and not too sweet.

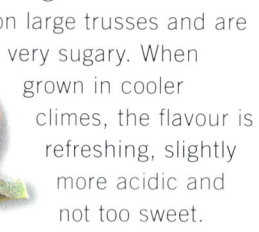

Below: Principe Borghese

PRUDEN'S PURPLE

Large and meaty, with few seeds, this recently rediscovered heirloom tomato resembles Brandywine, but ripens earlier on in the season. The dark pink fruit are globular, with deep pleats and can weigh anything from 225g/8oz to 450g/1lb. They look and taste good. Try them sliced in sandwiches with basil, or in salads. Alternatively, stuff them with fish or shellfish for a special Mediterranean-style treat.

Below: Pruden's Purple

Growth habits

Tomatoes grow in different ways. Bush types, which stop growing at a certain, predetermined height, do not need to be pruned or pinched out. This type of tomato is sometimes described as "determinate". Most of the fruit is produced over a four-week period. Determinate tomatoes benefit from some sort of support, to keep the fruit off the ground, but staking is not as vital as it is with the cordon or "indeterminate" tomatoes. If left to themselves, these tomatoes will go on growing and fruiting over a long period, although gardeners usually limit the growth to improve the size of the individual fruit, especially in colder climes. A third category, semi-bush tomatoes, are "determinate" but must be staked.

Below: Red Peach

RED PEACH

Like a peach, this early-ripening bush tomato has a fine fuzz or bloom on the skin. It is a deep orange/rose colour. The soft flesh has a mild, sweet flavour. There is also a yellow variety, which ripens to a pale, whitish/creamy colour, and whose flavour is even more intense.

Right: Red Pear

RED PEAR

Full of flavour, whether freshly picked or lightly cooked, this variety is particularly popular in the USA. The small fruits, which weigh around 25g/1oz, look like party light bulbs, and grow on strong, tall vines. They are well named, being decidedly pear shaped. There is also a yellow variety, which is equally popular but does not have quite such a rich taste. When sliced in half lengthways, these look pretty on a platter, especially when interleaved with basil and drizzled with dark green olive oil.

ROMA

A popular Italian plum tomato, this is a medium to late producing bush variety with large leaves. The scarlet fruits weigh around 50g/2oz each. If allowed to ripen on the bush, these tomatoes have a very good flavour. They have firm, thick flesh and very few seeds, so are very good cookers and are also often used for bottling.

Left: Rosadel

ROSADEL

This is one of a series (the Del series) of tomatoes bred by Lewis Darby, formerly in charge of tomato breeding at the Glasshouse Crops Research Institute in Britain. All are based on the popular Gardener's Delight, but are less prone to splitting. Rosadel is a dainty blush-pink cordon-type cherry tomato with a wonderful flavour. It fruits quite early on in the season.

RUFFLED

The name refers to the appearance of these tomatoes, the skin of which looks as though it has been tweaked into accordion pleats. The hollow seed cavity makes them perfect for stuffing, and they also look very attractive when hollowed out and filled with a salad. There are several varieties of ruffled tomatoes, both red and yellow.

Below: Roma

> ### Heirloom or heritage tomatoes
>
> These are old-fashioned varieties, often forgotten in the rush to find new and more commercially viable tomatoes. Unlike hybrids, the seeds produced from these tomatoes will produce the same fruiting characteristics as the parent plant. Traditionally, good gardeners have always saved seed and shared it with others. Now seed merchants are doing the same, so that we can all rediscover the tempting taste of traditional tomatoes that breed true.

Below: Ruffled

28 Guide to Tomato Varieties

SAN MARZANO

Similar to Roma, but larger and tastier, this is a good all-rounder, suitable for eating fresh in salads and sandwiches, but also ideal for sun-drying or bottling. Of Italian origin, it has been described as the original Italian tomato for sauces and pastes.

Above: San Marzano

> **Improving taste**
>
> The taste of a tomato depends on three main factors: the variety, the weather and the growing medium. Of all three, the natural quality and nutrient content of the soil makes a remarkable impact on flavour – after all, it is mostly from the roots that the tomatoes are fed. So enrich your soil and enjoy your harvest.

Above: Sun Belle

SUN BELLE

This small yellow tomato is shaped like a plum. It is noted for its exceptional flavour, and is high in both acid and sugar. A heavy cropper, it can be grown in cold or heated greenhouses. Enjoy it fresh in salads or salsas.

TIGERELLA

The name gives it away. This is another striped tomato (also known as Mr Stripey), and typically has greenish-yellow or orange broken stripes on a dark red background, which is largely lost on ripening. The small, round fruits are 4–5cm/1½–2in in diameter. A very early cordon-type, Tigerella can be grown outdoors or under glass. It has a tangy, almost tart flavour, and makes a good addition to salads.

Above: Yellow Butterfly

YELLOW BUTTERFLY

As pretty as its name suggests, this is a cordon-type tomato, producing 25g/1oz slightly pear-shaped cherry tomatoes, with a very sweet taste. It is an exceptionally heavy cropper, and grows best under glass. It makes an excellent cocktail snack if filled with soft cheese and chives, or, if you are feeling adventurous, it makes a surprising dessert if stewed with apples and sugar and made into a crumble (crisp).

Above: Supersweet 100

Above: Tigerella

Below: Tiny Tim

SUPERSWEET 100

A hybrid version of Gardener's Delight, this salad tomato is usually grown under glass. Each truss produces up to 100 bright red cherry tomatoes, each about 2cm/¾in in diameter. The flavour is sweet, rich and well balanced. It is claimed that the Supersweet 100 tomato is higher in Vitamin C than any other variety.

TINY TIM

Only about 2cm/¾in across, these tasty red dwarf tomatoes grow on decorative bush-type plants, which look good in tubs and hanging baskets. They are perfect for salads and as snacks. Tiny Tims also look attractive sliced on cocktail-size pizzas.

Guide to Tomato Varieties

Below: Yellow Cocktail

Above: Yellow Oxheart

Below: Wonder Light

Above: Yellow Currant

YELLOW OXHEART

Meaty and flavoursome, this is a bright yellow heart-shaped tomato, about 400–450g//14oz–1lb in weight. Like other oxhearts, it is a cordon type, with lacy foliage and few seeds.

YELLOW COCKTAIL

Chefs love this bright yellow pear-shaped miniature tomato, which has a good taste and makes a wonderful garnish. Fruits grown indoors are best, as the skin is more tender. The fruits also look good in salads and on kebabs, especially when alternated with red cherry tomatoes, thick slices of courgette (zucchini), aubergine (eggplant) and shallots.

YELLOW CURRANT

These pretty little tomatoes look good in pots and tubs. The plants on which they grow are highly ornamental, and bear extremely well. The tomatoes are reddish-orange in colour and have a pleasant, sweet flavour. Whole trusses of yellow currant look good as a table decoration. Piled in a bowl, they make delicious snacks, especially if you also offer a cream-cheese dip, flavoured with fresh herbs and spring onions (scallions).

WONDER LIGHT

A prolific producer, this bush tomato always needs staking, as the branches tend to bend under the weight of the 7.5cm/3in long oval lemon-yellow fruit. These tomatoes have a good rich flavour.

OTHER POPULAR VARIETIES

Amish Paste
An American heirloom tomato from Wisconsin. The 225g/8oz fruits are a cordon type and are large and elongated, with a deep red colour. Firm and meaty, with few seeds and low acidity, Amish Paste tomatoes are used for canning and for sauces.

Black Krim
For a dramatic effect, there are few tomatoes to equal this one. The skin is of such a deep tone of red that it often appears to be black, with a hint of dark green on the heavy shoulders. It comes from the Black Sea port of Krymsk and is sometimes known as Black Russian. The very large, slightly irregular fruits can weigh up to 350g/12oz and have maroon flesh, noted for its delicate, melting tenderness and rich, complex flavour.

Costoluto Fiorentino
An Italian beefsteak-type tomato, grown outdoors. The fruits are large, up to 10cm/4in in diameter, with irregular ribbing. They have a fleshy texture and exceptionally good flavour, and are ideal for stuffing, slicing and serving raw in salads.

Costoluto Genovese
A prolific variety from the Italian Riviera, first recorded in 1805. This scarlet, ribbed tomato is best grown in hot climates and is cultivated throughout the Mediterranean. These large, attractive fruits average about 200g/7oz. They have a meaty texture and are full-flavoured, with a hint of acidity. The ribbing ensures that they look good sliced in salads, but because of their meaty texture, they also cook well and make fine pasta sauces. They look very similar to Pruden's Purple, but are more deeply lobed.

The best soups are packed with flavour, and there's nothing better than a few ripe tomatoes to add that extra richness that makes a chilled soup such as Iced Tomato and Vodka Soup so special, or a warming Borlotti Bean and Pasta Soup so comforting. And what better way to start a meal than with the tangy flavour of juicy tomatoes? Try the delectable Tomato and Cheese Tarts or rustic Herby Polenta with Tomatoes; the possibilities are endless.

Soups and Snacks

32 Soups and Snacks

Iced Tomato AND Vodka Soup

This fresh-flavoured soup packs a punch like a frozen Bloody Mary. It is delicious served as an impressive first course for a summer's dinner party with sun-dried tomato bread.

SERVES FOUR

INGREDIENTS
   450g/1lb ripe, well-flavoured
      tomatoes, halved or
      roughly chopped
   600ml/1 pint/2½ cups jellied beef
      stock or consommé
   1 small red onion, halved
   2 celery sticks, cut into large pieces
   1 garlic clove, roughly chopped
   15ml/1 tbsp tomato purée (paste)
   10ml/2 tsp lemon juice
   10ml/2 tsp Worcestershire sauce
   a handful of small fresh basil leaves
   30ml/2 tbsp vodka
   salt and ground black pepper
   crushed ice, 4 small celery sticks and
      Sun-dried Tomato Bread, to serve

1 Put the halved or chopped tomatoes, jellied stock or consommé, onion and celery in a blender or food processor. Add the garlic, then spoon in the tomato purée. Pulse until all the vegetables are finely chopped, then process to a smooth paste.

2 Press the mixture through a sieve into a large bowl and stir in the lemon juice, Worcestershire sauce, basil leaves and vodka.

3 Add salt and pepper to taste. Cover and chill. Serve the soup with a little crushed ice and place a celery stick in each bowl.

COOK'S TIPS
• Canned beef consommé is ideal for this recipe, but vegetable stock, for vegetarians, will also work well.
• If you like, you can stand more celery sticks in a jug (pitcher) of iced water on the table for people to help themselves. The celery sticks can be used as additional edible stirrers and taste delicious after being dipped into the soup.
• Making your own sun-dried tomato bread is easy and is bound to impress your guests. If you don't have time, however, look out for tomato-flavoured ciabatta or focaccia.

Soups and Snacks 33

CHILLED TOMATO AND BASIL-FLOWER SOUP

THIS IS A REALLY FRESH-TASTING SOUP, PACKED WITH THE COMPLEMENTARY FLAVOURS OF TOMATO AND BASIL, AND TOPPED WITH PRETTY PINK AND PURPLE SWEET BASIL FLOWERS.

SERVES FOUR

INGREDIENTS
15ml/1 tbsp olive oil
1 onion, finely chopped
1 garlic clove, crushed
600ml/1 pint/2½ cups vegetable stock
900g/2lb tomatoes, roughly chopped
20 fresh basil leaves
a few drops of balsamic vinegar
juice of ½ lemon
150ml/¼ pint/⅔ cup natural (plain) yogurt
granulated sugar and salt, to taste
For the garnish
30ml/2 tbsp natural (plain) yogurt
8 small basil leaves
10ml/2 tsp basil flowers, all green parts removed

COOK'S TIP
Basil flowers may be small but they certainly have a beautifully aromatic flavour and are surprisingly sweet. They can be used fresh in all sorts of ways by being added with basil leaves to tomato salads or pizza toppings, sprinkled on pastas, or used as flavourings in tomato juice. To remove the flowers from the stem, simply pull – they will come away easily. Purple-leaved basil has a pretty mauve flower, which is delicious too.

1 Heat the oil in a pan and add the finely chopped onion and garlic. Fry the onion and garlic in the oil for 2–3 minutes until soft and transparent, stirring occasionally.

2 Add 300ml/½ pint/1¼ cups of the vegetable stock and the chopped tomatoes to the pan. Bring to the boil, then lower the heat and simmer the mixture for 15 minutes. Stir it occasionally to prevent it from sticking to the base of the pan.

3 Allow the mixture to cool slightly, then transfer it to a food processor and process until smooth. Press through a sieve placed over a bowl to remove the tomato skins and seeds.

4 Return the mixture to the food processor and add the remainder of the stock, half the basil leaves, the vinegar, lemon juice and yogurt. Season with sugar and salt to taste. Process until smooth. Pour into a bowl and chill.

5 Just before serving, finely shred the remaining basil leaves and add them to the soup. Pour the chilled soup into individual bowls. Garnish with yogurt topped with a few small basil leaves and a sprinkling of basil flowers.

Tomato and Fresh Basil Soup

A SOUP FOR LATE SUMMER WHEN FRESH TOMATOES ARE AT THEIR MOST FLAVOURSOME. SERVE WITH ONE OF THE MANY FLAVOURED BREADS YOU CAN BUY — A PESTO, OLIVE OR ROSEMARY LOAF WOULD GO PARTICULARLY WELL WITH THIS SOUP, OR SERVE WARM SODA BREAD.

SERVES FOUR TO SIX

INGREDIENTS
- 15ml/1 tbsp olive oil
- 25g/1oz/2 tbsp butter
- 1 medium onion, finely chopped
- 900g/2lb ripe plum tomatoes, chopped
- 1 garlic clove, chopped
- 750ml/1¼ pints/3 cups chicken stock
- 120ml/4fl oz/½ cup dry white wine
- 30ml/2 tbsp sun-dried tomato purée (paste)
- 30ml/2 tbsp shredded fresh basil
- 150ml/¼ pint/⅔ cup double (heavy) cream
- salt and ground black pepper
- fresh basil, to garnish

1 Heat the oil and butter in a large pan until foaming. Add the onion and cook gently for about 5 minutes, stirring frequently with a wooden spoon, until softened but not brown.

2 Stir in the chopped tomatoes and garlic, then add the stock, wine and sun-dried tomato purée, with salt and pepper to taste. Bring to the boil, then lower the heat, half cover the pan and simmer gently for 20 minutes, stirring occasionally to stop the tomatoes sticking to the base of the pan.

3 Process the soup with the shredded basil in a blender or food processor, then press through a sieve into a clean pan.

4 Add the double cream and heat through very gently, stirring. Do not allow the soup to overheat. Check the consistency and add a little more stock or water if necessary, then taste for seasoning. Pour into heated bowls and garnish with basil. Serve at once.

VARIATION
This soup can also be served chilled. Pour it into a container after sieving, allow to cool to room temperature and then chill in the refrigerator for at least 4 hours. Serve in chilled bowls.

Roasted Garlic and Butternut Squash Soup with Tomato Salsa

This is a wonderful, richly-flavoured dish. A spoonful of the hot and spicy tomato salsa gives bite to the sweet-tasting squash and garlic soup.

SERVES FOUR TO FIVE

INGREDIENTS
- 2 garlic bulbs, outer papery skin removed
- a few fresh thyme sprigs
- 75ml/5 tbsp olive oil
- 1 large butternut squash, halved and seeded
- 2 onions, chopped
- 5ml/1 tsp ground coriander
- 1.2 litres/2 pints/5 cups vegetable or chicken stock
- 30–45ml/2–3 tbsp chopped fresh oregano or marjoram
- salt and ground black pepper

For the salsa
- 4 large ripe tomatoes, halved and seeded
- 1 red (bell) pepper, seeded
- 1 large fresh red chilli, halved and seeded
- 30ml/2 tbsp extra virgin olive oil
- 15ml/1 tbsp balsamic vinegar
- pinch of caster (superfine) sugar

1 Preheat the oven to 220°C/425°F/Gas 7. Place the garlic bulbs on a piece of foil, add the thyme and drizzle over half the olive oil, then fold the foil around the garlic bulbs to enclose them.

2 Transfer the foil parcel to a baking sheet with the butternut squash and brush the squash with 15ml/1 tbsp of the remaining olive oil. Place the tomatoes, red pepper and fresh chilli for the salsa on the baking sheet.

3 Roast the vegetables for 25 minutes, then remove the tomatoes, pepper and chilli. Reduce the temperature to 190°C/375°F/Gas 5 and cook the squash and garlic for 20–25 minutes more, or until the squash is tender.

4 Heat the remaining oil in a large, heavy pan and cook the onions and ground coriander gently for about 10 minutes, or until softened and just beginning to brown.

5 Meanwhile, skin the pepper and chilli, then process them in a food processor or blender with the tomatoes and the olive oil for the salsa. Stir in the balsamic vinegar and seasoning to taste, adding a pinch of caster sugar, if necessary, to moderate the taste.

6 Squeeze the roasted garlic out of its papery skin into the onions and scoop the squash out of its skin, adding it to the pan too. Add the stock, 5ml/1 tsp salt and plenty of black pepper. Bring to the boil, then simmer for 10 minutes.

7 Stir in half the fresh oregano or marjoram and cool the soup slightly before processing it in a blender or food processor. Alternatively, use a wooden spoon to press the soup through a fine sieve placed over a bowl.

8 Reheat the soup without allowing it to boil, then taste for seasoning before ladling it into warmed bowls. Top each with a spoonful of salsa and sprinkle with the remaining chopped oregano or marjoram. Serve immediately.

PISTOU

A delicious chunky vegetable soup from Nice in the south of France, served with a tomato pesto, and fresh Parmesan cheese. Serve in small portions as an appetizer, or in larger bowls with crusty bread as a filling lunch.

SERVES FOUR TO SIX

INGREDIENTS
- 1 courgette (zucchini), diced
- 1 small potato, diced
- 1 shallot, chopped
- 1 carrot, diced
- 400g/14oz can chopped tomatoes
- 1.2 litres/2 pints/5 cups vegetable stock
- 50g/2oz green beans, cut into 1cm/½in lengths
- 50g/2oz/½ cup frozen petits pois (baby peas)
- 50g/2oz/½ cup small pasta shapes
- 60–90ml/4–6 tbsp pesto
- 15ml/1 tbsp tomato purée (paste)
- salt and ground black pepper
- freshly grated Parmesan or Pecorino cheese, to serve

1 Place the courgette, potato, shallot, carrot and tomatoes, with the can juices, in a large pan. Add the vegetable stock and season with salt and plenty of ground black pepper. Bring to the boil over a medium to high heat, then lower the heat, cover the pan and simmer for 20 minutes.

2 Bring the soup back to the boil and add the green beans and petits pois to the pan. Cook the mixture briefly, for about a minute.

VARIATION
To strengthen the tomato flavour, try using tomato-flavoured spaghetti, broken into small lengths, instead of the small pasta shapes. Sun-dried tomato purée (paste) can be used instead of regular.

3 Add the pasta. Cook the mixture for a further 10 minutes, until the pasta is tender. Taste and adjust the seasoning.

4 Ladle the soup into bowls. Mix together the pesto and tomato purée, and stir a spoonful into each serving. Sprinkle with freshly grated cheese.

Ribollita

THIS SOUP IS RATHER LIKE AN ITALIAN MINESTRONE. IT IS BASED ON TOMATOES, BUT WITH BEANS INSTEAD OF PASTA. IN ITALY IT IS TRADITIONALLY LADLED OVER BREAD AND A GREEN VEGETABLE.

SERVES SIX TO EIGHT

INGREDIENTS
- 350g/12oz well-flavoured tomatoes, preferably plum tomatoes
- 45ml/3 tbsp extra virgin olive oil or sunflower oil
- 2 onions, chopped
- 2 carrots, sliced
- 4 garlic cloves, crushed
- 2 celery sticks, thinly sliced
- 1 fennel bulb, trimmed and chopped
- 2 large courgettes (zucchini), thinly sliced
- 400g/14oz can chopped tomatoes
- 30ml/2 tbsp pesto
- 900ml/1½ pints/3¾ cups vegetable stock
- 400g/14oz can haricot (navy) or borlotti beans, drained
- salt and ground black pepper

To finish
- 15ml/1 tbsp extra virgin olive oil, plus extra for drizzling
- 450g/1lb fresh young spinach
- 6–8 slices white bread
- Parmesan or Pecorino cheese shavings

1 To skin the tomatoes, plunge them into boiling water for 30 seconds, refresh in cold water and then peel off the skins. Chop the tomato flesh and set it aside.

2 Heat the oil in a large pan. Add the onions, carrots, garlic, celery and fennel and fry gently for 10 minutes. Add the courgettes and fry for a further 2 minutes.

3 Stir in the chopped fresh and canned tomatoes, pesto, stock and beans, and bring to the boil. Lower the heat, cover the pan and simmer gently for 25–30 minutes, until the vegetables are completely tender and the stock is full of flavour. Season the soup with salt and pepper to taste.

4 To finish, heat the oil in a frying pan and fry the spinach for 2 minutes or until wilted. Place a slice of bread in each serving bowl, top with the spinach and then ladle the soup over the spinach. Serve with extra olive oil for drizzling on to the soup, and Parmesan cheese to sprinkle on top.

Borlotti Bean and Pasta Soup

A complete meal in a bowl, this is a version of a classic Italian soup. Traditionally, the person who finds the bay leaf is honoured with a kiss from the cook.

SERVES FOUR

INGREDIENTS
- 1 onion, chopped
- 1 celery stick, chopped
- 2 carrots, chopped
- 75ml/5 tbsp olive oil
- 1 bay leaf
- 1 glass white wine (optional)
- 1 litre/1¾ pints/4 cups vegetable stock
- 400g/14oz can chopped tomatoes
- 300ml/½ pint/1¼ cups passata (bottled strained tomatoes)
- 175g/6oz/1½ cups dried pasta shapes, such as farfalle or conchiglie
- 400g/14oz can borlotti beans, drained
- salt and ground black pepper
- 250g/9oz spinach, washed and drained
- 50g/2oz/⅔ cup freshly grated Parmesan cheese, to serve

VARIATION
Other beans, such as cannellini beans, haricot (navy) beans or chickpeas, are equally good in this soup.

1 Place the chopped onion, celery and carrots in a large pan with the olive oil. Cook over a medium heat for 5 minutes or until the vegetables soften, stirring occasionally.

2 Add the bay leaf, wine, vegetable stock, tomatoes and passata, and bring to the boil. Lower the heat and simmer for 10 minutes until the vegetables are just tender.

3 Add the pasta and beans, and bring the soup back to the boil, then simmer for 8 minutes until the pasta is *al dente*. Stir frequently to prevent the pasta from sticking.

4 Season to taste with salt and pepper. Remove any thick stalks from the spinach and add it to the mixture. Cook for a further 2 minutes. Serve in heated soup bowls sprinkled with the freshly grated Parmesan.

VARIATIONS
- This soup is also delicious with chunks of cooked spicy sausage or pieces of crispy cooked pancetta or bacon – simply add to the soup at the end of Step 3 and stir in, ensuring that the meat is piping hot before serving.
- For vegetarians, you could use fried chunks of smoked or marinated tofu as an alternative to meat.

Moroccan Harira

This is a hearty main-course meat and vegetable soup, eaten during the month of Ramadan, when the Muslim population fasts between sunrise and sunset.

SERVES FOUR

INGREDIENTS
- 450g/1lb well-flavoured tomatoes
- 225g/8oz lamb, cut into pieces
- 2.5ml/½ tsp ground turmeric
- 2.5ml/½ tsp ground cinnamon
- 25g/1oz/2 tbsp butter
- 60ml/4 tbsp chopped fresh coriander (cilantro)
- 30ml/2 tbsp chopped fresh parsley
- 1 onion, chopped
- 50g/2oz/¼ cup split red lentils
- 75g/3oz/½ cup dried chickpeas, soaked overnight in cold water
- 600ml/1 pint/2½ cups water
- 4 baby (pearl) onions or shallots
- 25g/1oz/¼ cup fine noodles
- salt and ground black pepper
- fresh coriander (cilantro), lemon slices and ground cinnamon, to garnish

COOK'S TIPS
- Most of the vitamins in fruits and vegetables are just under the skin. So, if you wish to improve the nutritional content, or simply save some time, the skins of the tomatoes can be left on.
- For maximum cinnamon flavour, grind a broken cinnamon stick in a spice grinder or a coffee grinder kept especially for the purpose.

1 Plunge the tomatoes into boiling water for 30 seconds, then refresh in cold water. Peel off the skins. Cut into quarters and remove the seeds. Chop the flesh roughly.

2 Put the pieces of lamb, ground turmeric, cinnamon, butter, fresh coriander, parsley and onion into a large pan, and cook over a medium heat, stirring, for 5 minutes.

3 Add the chopped tomatoes and continue to cook for 10 minutes, stirring the mixture frequently.

4 Rinse the lentils under running water and drain them well. Stir them into the contents of the pan, with the drained chickpeas and the measured water. Season with salt and pepper. Bring to the boil, lower the heat, cover, and simmer gently for 1½ hours.

5 Add the onions or shallots. Cook for 25 minutes. Add the noodles and cook for 5 minutes more. Spoon into bowls and garnish with the coriander, lemon slices and cinnamon.

Seafood Soup with Rouille

This is a really chunky, aromatic mixed fish and tomato soup from France, flavoured with plenty of saffron and herbs. Rouille, a fiery hot paste, is served separately for everyone to swirl into their soup to flavour.

SERVES FOUR

INGREDIENTS

- 3 gurnard, red mullet or snapper, scaled and gutted
- 12 large prawns (shrimp)
- 675g/1½lb white fish, such as cod, haddock, halibut or monkfish
- 225g/8oz live mussels
- 1 onion, quartered
- 600ml/1 pint/2½ cups vegetable stock
- 5ml/1 tsp saffron threads
- 75ml/5 tbsp olive oil
- 1 fennel bulb, roughly chopped
- 4 garlic cloves, crushed
- 3 strips pared orange rind
- 4 fresh thyme sprigs
- 900g/2lb tomatoes
- 30ml/2 tbsp sun-dried tomato purée (paste)
- 3 bay leaves

For the rouille
- 1 red (bell) pepper, seeded
- 1 fresh red chilli, seeded and sliced
- 2 garlic cloves, chopped
- 75ml/5 tbsp olive oil
- 15g/½oz/¼ cup fresh breadcrumbs

1 To make the rouille, process the pepper, chilli, garlic, oil and breadcrumbs in a blender or food processor until smooth. Transfer to a serving dish and chill.

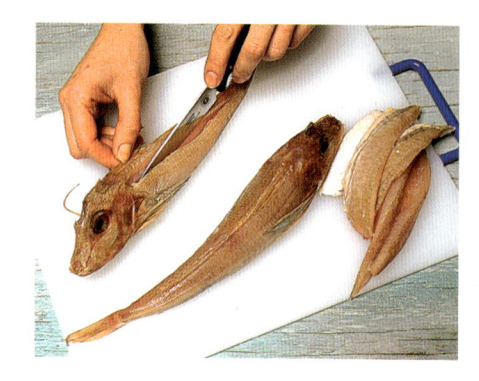

2 Fillet the gurnard, mullet or snapper by cutting away the flesh from either side of the backbone, reserving the heads and bones for the stock.

3 Cut the fillets into small chunks. Shell half the prawns and reserve the trimmings to make the fish stock.

4 Skin the white fish, discarding any bones, and cut into large chunks. Scrub the mussels well, discarding any damaged ones and any open ones that do not close when sharply tapped.

5 To make the stock, put the fish and prawn trimmings in a pan with the onion and the water. Bring to the boil, then simmer gently for 30 minutes. Cool slightly and strain.

6 Soak the saffron in 600ml/1 pint/2½ cups hot vegetable stock. Heat 30ml/2 tbsp of the oil in a large sauté pan. Add all the fish and fry over a high heat for 1 minute. Drain and set aside.

7 Heat the remaining oil and fry the fennel, garlic, orange rind and thyme until beginning to colour. Make up the strained stock to about 1.2 litres/2 pints/5 cups with the vegetable stock.

8 Skin the tomatoes by plunging them into boiling water for 30 seconds, then refreshing them in cold water. Peel and chop. Add the stock to the pan with the saffron, tomatoes, tomato purée and bay leaves. Season, bring almost to the boil, then simmer gently, covered, for 20 minutes.

9 Stir in the gurnard, mullet or snapper, white fish and prawns, and add the mussels. Cover the pan tightly and cook for 3–4 minutes. Remove from the heat and take off the lid. Discard any mussels that do not open. Serve the soup piping hot with the rouille served separately in a small dish.

COOK'S TIPS
- To save time, order the fish and ask the fishmonger to fillet the gurnard or mullet for you.
- To temper the flavour of the rouille, blend a chopped tomato with the other ingredients or leave out the fresh chilli.

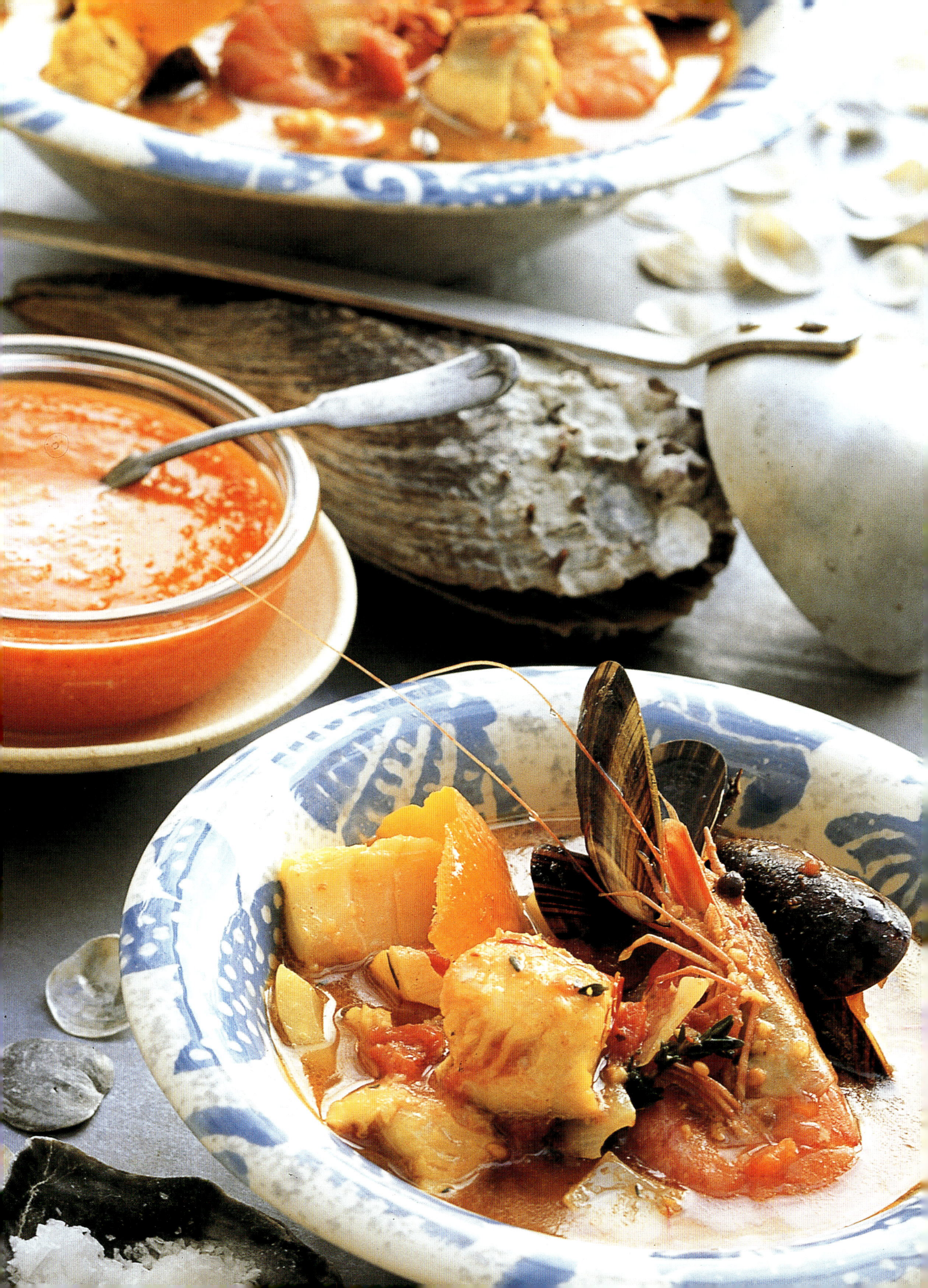

Provençal Fish Soup

The addition of rice makes this a substantial main meal soup. Basmati or Thai rice are delicious, if you can find them, but any long grain rice could be used. If you prefer a stronger tomato flavour, replace the white wine with extra passata.

SERVES FOUR TO SIX

INGREDIENTS
- 450g/1lb fresh mussels
- about 250ml/8fl oz/1 cup white wine
- 675–900g/1½–2lb mixed white fish fillets such as monkfish, plaice, flounder, cod or haddock
- 6 large scallops
- 30ml/2 tbsp olive oil
- 3 leeks, chopped
- 1 garlic clove, crushed
- 1 red (bell) pepper, seeded and cut into 2.5cm/1in pieces
- 1 yellow (bell) pepper, seeded and cut into 2.5cm/1in pieces
- 175g/6oz fennel bulb, cut into 4cm/1½in pieces
- 400g/14oz can chopped tomatoes
- 150ml/¼ pint/⅔ cup passata (bottled strained tomatoes)
- about 1 litre/1¾ pints/4 cups well-flavoured fish stock
- generous pinch of saffron threads, soaked in 15ml/1 tbsp hot water
- 175g/6oz/scant 1 cup basmati rice, soaked
- 8 large raw prawns (shrimp), peeled and deveined
- salt and ground black pepper
- 30–45ml/2–3 tbsp fresh dill, to garnish

1 Clean the mussels, discarding any that do not close when tapped with a knife. Place them in a heavy pan. Add 90ml/6 tbsp of the wine, cover, bring to the boil over a high heat and cook for about 3 minutes or until all the mussels have opened.

2 Strain, reserving the liquid. Discard any mussels that have not opened. Set aside half the mussels in their shells for the garnish; shell the rest and put them in a bowl.

3 Cut the fish into 2.5cm/1in cubes. Detach the corals from the scallops and slice the white flesh into three or four pieces. Add the scallops to the fish and the corals to the shelled mussels.

4 Heat the olive oil in a pan and fry the leeks and garlic for 3–4 minutes, until softened. Add the pepper chunks and fennel, and fry for 2 minutes more until just softened.

COOK'S TIP
To make your own fish stock, place about 450g/1lb white fish trimmings – bones, heads, but not gills – in a large pan. Add a chopped onion, carrot, bay leaf, parsley sprig, 6 peppercorns and a piece of pared lemon rind. Pour in 1.2 litres/2 pints/5 cups water, bring to the boil, then simmer gently for 25–30 minutes. Strain through muslin (cheesecloth).

5 Add the tomatoes, passata, stock, saffron water, mussel liquid and wine. Season and cook for 5 minutes. Drain the rice, stir it into the mixture, cover and simmer for 10 minutes.

6 Carefully stir in the white fish and cook over a low heat for 5 minutes. Add the prawns, cook for 2 minutes, then add the scallop corals and shelled mussels and cook for 2–3 minutes more, until all the fish is tender. Add a little extra white wine or stock if needed. Spoon into warmed soup dishes, top with mussels in their shells and sprinkle with the dill. Serve immediately.

Mediterranean Leek and Fish Soup with Tomatoes and Garlic

This chunky soup, which is almost a stew, makes a robust and wonderfully aromatic meal in a bowl. Serve it with crisp-baked croûtes spread with a tasty, garlic mayonnaise.

SERVES FOUR

INGREDIENTS

- 2 large thick leeks
- 30ml/2 tbsp olive oil
- 5ml/1 tsp crushed coriander seeds
- a good pinch of dried red chilli flakes
- 300g/11oz small salad potatoes, peeled and thickly sliced
- 400g/14oz can chopped tomatoes
- 600ml/1 pint/2½ cups fish stock
- 150ml/¼ pint/⅔ cup white wine
- 1 fresh bay leaf
- 1 star anise
- strip of pared orange rind
- good pinch of saffron threads
- 450g/1lb white fish fillets, such as monkfish, sea bass, cod or haddock
- 450g/1lb small squid, cleaned
- 250g/9oz raw peeled prawns (shrimp)
- 30–45ml/2–3 tbsp chopped flat leaf parsley
- salt and ground black pepper

To serve
- 1 short French loaf, sliced and toasted
- garlic mayonnaise

1 Slice the leeks, keeping the green tops separate from the white bottom pieces. Wash the leek slices thoroughly in a colander and drain them well. Set the white slices aside for later.

2 Heat the oil in a heavy pan over a low heat, then add the green leek slices, the crushed coriander seeds and the dried red chilli flakes. Cook, stirring occasionally, for 5 minutes.

3 Add the potatoes and tomatoes, and pour in the stock and wine. Add the bay leaf, star anise, orange rind and saffron. Bring to the boil, lower the heat and partially cover the pan. Simmer for 20 minutes or until the potatoes are tender. Taste and adjust the seasoning.

4 Cut the white fish fillets into chunks. Cut the squid sacs into rectangles and score a criss-cross pattern into them without cutting right through.

5 Add the fish to the soup and cook gently for 4 minutes. Add the prawns and cook for 1 minute. Add the squid and the sliced white part of the leek and cook, stirring occasionally, for a further 2 minutes.

6 Finally, stir in the chopped parsley and serve immediately, ladling the soup into warmed bowls. Offer the toasted French bread and the garlic mayonnaise with the soup.

Scrambled Eggs

This dish is a speciality of northern Iran where it is called Mirza Ghasemi. *Serve it with warm pitta bread for a colourful and most unusual first course.*

SERVES FOUR TO SIX

INGREDIENTS

4 aubergines (eggplant)
115g/4oz/½ cup butter
1 large onion, finely chopped
2 garlic cloves, crushed
4 large tomatoes, peeled, seeded and chopped
4 eggs, beaten
salt and ground black pepper
warm pitta bread, to serve

COOK'S TIP
Small pitta breads can be used as scoops for the delicious aubergine and egg mixture; alternatively, open up the pockets in larger pitta breads and fill them with the mixture. For a delicious change, use ciabatta, panini, rustic brown bread or sun-dried tomato and olive bread as a scoop.

1 Preheat the oven to 190°C/375°F/Gas 5. Carefully score the skins of the aubergines with a sharp knife, place them on a baking sheet and bake in the oven for 30–40 minutes until the skins begin to split open.

2 Meanwhile, melt 50g/2oz/¼ cup of the butter in a large frying pan and fry the onion and garlic for 4–5 minutes until softened. Add the tomatoes and fry for a further 2–3 minutes.

3 Peel the aubergines, finely chop the flesh and stir it into the pan with the onion and tomatoes. Cook for about 4–5 minutes, stirring frequently.

4 Melt the remaining butter in a small frying pan, add the beaten eggs and cook over a low heat until the eggs are just beginning to set, stirring occasionally with a wooden spoon. Stir the eggs into the aubergine mixture, season and serve with pitta bread.

TOMATO AND CHEESE TARTS

These crisp little tartlets look really impressive but are actually very easy to make. They are best eaten fresh from the oven and make ideal snacks with drinks.

SERVES FOUR

INGREDIENTS
 2 sheets filo pastry
 cornflour (cornstarch),
  for dusting
 1 egg white
 115g/4oz/½ cup cream cheese
 a handful of fresh basil leaves
 4 tomatoes, sliced
 salt and ground black pepper

VARIATIONS
• For a stronger cheese taste, sprinkle the tartlets with grated Cheddar or Parmesan cheese or top with a slice of mozzarella cheese before baking.

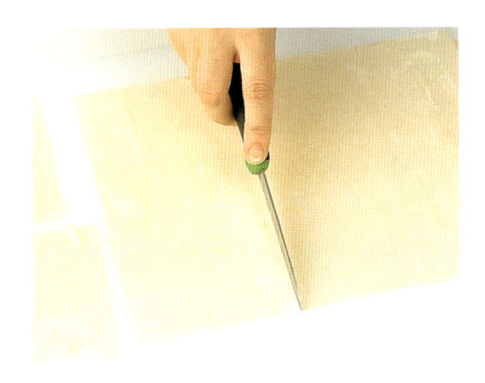

1 Preheat the oven to 200°C/400°F/Gas 6. Lay out the filo pastry on a board dusted with cornflour (cornstarch). Brush the sheets of filo pastry lightly with egg white and cut into 16 10cm/4in squares.

2 Layer the squares in twos, in a tartlet tin (muffin pan). Divide the cheese among the pastry cases. Season with black pepper and top with a few basil leaves.

3 Arrange the tomato slices on the cheese, season well and bake the tarts for 10–12 minutes, until golden and crisp. Serve warm.

COOK'S TIPS
• When you are using filo pastry it is important to prevent it from drying out; cover any you are not using with a dishtowel or clear film (plastic wrap).
• Using egg white to brush the sheets of filo is quite unusual, but makes a change from the traditional – and much richer – melted butter. Of course, you can use butter if you prefer, but if you like the low-fat option, stick to the egg white and use a low-fat cream cheese.
• These tartlets are delicious served with chutney or salsa. Alternatively, serve with pesto mayonnaise – mix 90ml/6 tbsp mayonnaise into 15ml/1 tbsp pesto.

Roasted Tomato and Mozzarella with Basil Oil and Mixed Leaf Salad

Roasting the tomatoes in olive oil adds a new dimension to this delicious dish and a superb sweetness to the tomatoes. Make the basil oil just before serving to retain its fresh flavour and vivid emerald-green colour.

SERVES FOUR

INGREDIENTS
- olive oil, for brushing
- 6 large plum tomatoes
- 350g/12oz fresh mozzarella cheese, cut into 8–12 slices
- fresh basil leaves, to garnish

For the basil oil
- 25 fresh basil leaves
- 60ml/4 tbsp extra virgin olive oil
- 1 garlic clove, crushed

For the salad
- 90g/3½oz/4 cups salad leaves
- 50g/2oz/2 cups mixed salad herbs, such as coriander (cilantro), basil and rocket (arugula)
- 25g/1oz/3 tbsp pumpkin seeds
- 25g/1oz/3 tbsp sunflower seeds

For the salad dressing
- 60ml/4tbsp extra virgin olive oil
- 15ml/1 tbsp balsamic vinegar
- 2.5 ml/½ tsp Dijon mustard

1 Preheat the oven to 200°C/400°F/Gas 6 and oil a baking sheet. Cut the tomatoes in half lengthwise and remove the seeds. Place skin-side down on a baking sheet and roast for 20 minutes or until the tomatoes are tender.

2 Meanwhile, make the basil oil. Place the basil leaves, olive oil and garlic in a food processor and process until smooth. Transfer to a bowl and chill.

3 Start to prepare the salad. Put the salad leaves in a large bowl. Add the mixed salad herbs and toss lightly with your hands to mix.

4 Toast the pumpkin and sunflower seeds in a dry frying pan over a medium heat for 2 minutes until golden, tossing frequently. Let the seeds cool before sprinkling them over the salad.

5 To make the salad dressing, combine the ingredients in a screw-top jar or bowl. Shake or mix with a small whisk or fork until combined. Pour the dressing over the salad and toss with your hands until the leaves are well coated.

6 For each serving, place the tomato halves on top of 2 or 3 slices of mozzarella and drizzle over the basil oil. Season well. Garnish with basil leaves. Serve with the salad.

Soups and Snacks 47

Herby Polenta with Tomatoes

Golden polenta flavoured with a selection of fresh summer herbs is pan-fried with seasonal tomatoes for a delicious taste of northern Italian cuisine.

SERVES FOUR

INGREDIENTS
750ml/1¼ pints/3 cups vegetable stock or water
5ml/1 tsp salt
175g/6oz/1 cup polenta
25g/1oz/2 tbsp butter
75ml/5 tbsp chopped mixed fresh parsley, thyme, chives and basil, plus extra, to garnish
olive oil, for greasing and brushing
6 large plum or beefsteak tomatoes
salt and ground black pepper

COOK'S TIPS
• To get the criss-cross effect on the polenta, turn each round through 90 degrees, halfway through cooking each side on the griddle pan.
• Any mixture of fresh herbs can be used, or try using just basil or chives alone, for a really distinctive flavour. Garlic chives taste very good.
• If you like garlic, simply add one minced (ground) clove when adding the rest of the herbs.

1 Prepare the polenta in advance: place the stock or water in a heavy pan, with the salt, and bring to the boil. Lower the heat, slowly pour in the polenta and stir with a wooden spoon.

2 Stir the mixture constantly, using a figure-eight action, over a medium heat for 5 minutes, until the polenta begins to thicken and come away from the sides of the pan.

3 Remove from the heat and continue stirring for another minute or two. Stir in the butter, freshly chopped parsley, thyme, chives and basil, and season with black pepper.

4 Tip the mixture into a wide, greased tin (pan) or a glass or ceramic dish. Using a flexible spatula, spread the polenta mixture out evenly. Cover the surface closely with greaseproof (waxed) paper, then put it in a cool place until it has set completely and is cold.

5 Turn out the polenta on to a board and stamp out 8 rounds using a large biscuit or cookie cutter. Alternatively, you can cut the polenta into 8 squares with a knife. Brush with oil.

6 Heat a griddle pan and lightly brush it with oil. Cut the tomatoes in two, then brush them with oil and sprinkle with salt and pepper. Cook the tomato halves and polenta patties on the pan for 5 minutes, turning them once. Serve garnished with fresh herbs.

Cannellini Bean and Tomato Bruschetta

This traditional Italian-style dish is a sophisticated version of beans on toast. The beans add flavour while making this appetizer more substantial.

SERVES FOUR

INGREDIENTS

- 150g/5oz/¾ cup dried cannellini beans
- 5 tomatoes
- 45ml/3 tbsp olive oil, plus extra for drizzling
- 2 sun-dried tomatoes in oil, drained and finely chopped
- 2 garlic cloves
- 30ml/2 tbsp chopped fresh rosemary
- 12 slices Italian-style bread, such as ciabatta
- salt and ground black pepper
- a handful of fresh basil leaves, to garnish

VARIATION
Bruschetta can be served with a variety of toppings. Make the tomato base as in steps 2 and 3 and mix with canned, flaked tuna, olives or pieces of cooked ham instead of the beans.

1 Soak the beans in water overnight. Drain and rinse the beans, then place in a pan and cover with fresh water. Bring to the boil and boil rapidly for 10 minutes. Reduce the heat and simmer for 50–60 minutes or until tender. Drain and return to the clean pan.

2 Meanwhile, place the tomatoes in a bowl, cover with boiling water, leave for 30 seconds, then refresh in cold water. Peel, seed and chop the flesh.

3 Heat the oil in a pan and add the fresh and sun-dried tomatoes. Crush 1 garlic clove and add it with the rosemary. Cook for 2 minutes until the tomatoes begin to break down.

4 Add the tomato mixture to the cooked cannellini beans, season to taste with salt and ground pepper, and mix well. Heat through gently.

5 Cut the remaining garlic clove in half and rub the cut sides of the bread slices with it. Toast the bread lightly. Spoon the cannellini bean mixture on top of the toast. Sprinkle with basil leaves and drizzle with a little extra olive oil before serving.

COOK'S TIP
Canned beans can be used instead of dried; use 275g/10oz/2 cups drained, canned beans and add to the tomato mixture in step 4. If the beans are canned in brine, then rinse and drain them well before use.

Pipérade with Crostini

This mixture of ripe plum tomatoes, sweet peppers and eggs has all the flavours of the Mediterranean. It is perfect for a tasty appetizer or a light lunch-time snack.

SERVES SIX

INGREDIENTS
- 60ml/4 tbsp bacon fat, duck fat or olive oil
- 2 small onions, coarsely chopped
- 4 red or yellow (bell) peppers, seeded and chopped
- 2 large garlic cloves, finely chopped
- pinch of chilli powder
- 675g/1½lb ripe plum tomatoes, peeled, seeded and chopped
- 15ml/1 tbsp chopped fresh oregano or 5ml/1 tsp dried oregano
- 1 long French stick
- 60–90ml/4–6 tbsp olive oil
- 25g/1oz/2 tbsp butter
- 6 eggs, beaten
- salt and ground black pepper
- fresh basil leaves, to serve

VARIATION
To make a quick party version, cut the bread into thick slices and mix about 200ml/7fl oz/scant 1 cup ready-made sweet pepper and tomato pasta sauce into the eggs in Step 4.

1 Heat the fat or oil in a large, heavy frying pan. Add the onions and cook over a gentle heat, stirring occasionally, for about 5 minutes until softened but not coloured.

2 Add the peppers, garlic and chilli powder. Cook for a further 5 minutes, stirring, then add the plum tomatoes, seasoning and oregano, and cook over a medium heat for 15–20 minutes until most of the liquid has evaporated.

3 Preheat the oven to 200°C/400°F/Gas 6. Cut the bread in half lengthways, trim off the ends, then cut into six equal pieces and brush with olive oil. Place on baking sheets; bake for 8–10 minutes until crisp and just turning golden.

4 Heat the butter until it bubbles, add the eggs and stir until soft scrambled. Turn off the heat and stir in the tomato mixture. Divide evenly among the pieces of bread and sprinkle with the basil leaves. Serve hot or warm.

Mozzarella and Tomato Skewers

STACKS OF FLAVOUR — LAYERS OF OVEN-BAKED MOZZARELLA, TOMATOES, BASIL AND BREAD. THESE COLOURFUL KEBABS WILL BE POPULAR WITH ADULTS AND CHILDREN ALIKE.

SERVES FOUR

INGREDIENTS
- 12 slices white country bread, each about 1cm/½in thick
- 45ml/3 tbsp olive oil
- 225g/8oz mozzarella cheese, cut into 5mm/¼in slices
- 3 ripe plum tomatoes, cut into 5mm/¼in slices
- 15g/½oz/½ cup fresh basil leaves, plus extra to garnish
- salt and ground black pepper
- 30ml/2 tbsp chopped fresh flat leaf parsley, to garnish

COOK'S TIPS
- If you use wooden skewers, soak them in water first, to prevent them from scorching during the cooking time.
- The bread for these skewers needs to be quite robust, so don't be tempted to use slices from a soft white sandwich loaf.

1 Preheat the oven to 220°C/425°F/Gas 7. Trim the crusts from the bread and cut each slice into four equal squares. Arrange on a baking sheet and brush with half the olive oil. Bake for 3–5 minutes until the squares are a pale golden colour.

2 Remove the bread squares from the oven and place them on a chopping board with the other ingredients.

3 Make 16 stacks, each starting with a square of bread, then a slice of mozzarella topped with a slice of tomato and a basil leaf. Sprinkle with salt and pepper, then repeat, ending with a piece of bread. Push a skewer through each stack and place on the baking sheet. Drizzle with the remaining oil and bake for 10–15 minutes until the cheese begins to melt. Garnish with basil and flat leaf parsley.

Tostadas with Tomato Salsa

A tostada is a crisp, fried tortilla used in this recipe as a base on which to pile the topping of your choice. This variation on a sandwich makes a very tasty snack.

SERVES SIX

INGREDIENTS

   30ml/2 tbsp oil, plus extra
     for frying
   1 onion, chopped
   2 garlic cloves, chopped
   2.5ml/½ tsp chilli powder
   400g/14oz can borlotti or pinto
     beans, drained
   150ml/¼ pint/⅔ cup chicken stock
   15ml/1 tbsp tomato purée (paste)
   30ml/2 tbsp chopped fresh
     coriander (cilantro)
   6 wheat or corn tortillas
   30ml/2 tbsp sour cream
   50g/2oz/½ cup grated
     Cheddar cheese
   salt and ground black pepper
   6 sprigs of fresh coriander,
     to garnish
For the tomato salsa
   1 small onion, chopped
   1 garlic clove, crushed
   2 fresh green chillies, seeded and
     finely chopped
   450g/1lb tomatoes, chopped
   30ml/2 tbsp chopped fresh
     coriander (cilantro)

1 To make the salsa, put the onion and garlic in a serving bowl and stir in the chillies, tomatoes and fresh coriander. Season generously and mix well.

2 Heat 30ml/2 tbsp oil in a heavy-based frying pan and fry the chopped onion for 3–5 minutes until softened. Add the garlic and chilli powder, and fry for 1 minute, stirring constantly.

3 Add the beans. Pour in the stock and mix well. Mash the beans very roughly. Add the tomato purée, chopped coriander and seasoning to taste. Mix thoroughly and cook for a few minutes.

4 Fry 2 tortillas in hot oil for 1 minute, turning once, until crisp, then drain on kitchen paper. Fry the remaining tortillas in the same way.

5 Put a spoonful of the refried beans on each tostada, spoon over some tomato salsa, then some sour cream, sprinkle with grated Cheddar cheese and garnish with coriander.

COOK'S TIP
When you are in a hurry, use canned refried beans. Thin them with a little stock if necessary.

Tomatoes are just as delicious raw or cooked, so it is hardly surprising that they are used all over the world to add a splash of colour as well as a delicious flavour to an astonishingly wide variety of dishes. Cherry tomatoes add a sweet tangy bite to Country Pasta Salad while beefsteaks give a meaty texture to refreshing Mango, Tomato and Red Onion Salad. And if there's a glut of tomatoes, what better way to use them than in dishes such as Marquis Potatoes, or Okra with Coriander and Tomatoes?

Side Dishes and Salads

Okra with Coriander and Tomatoes

OKRA IS FREQUENTLY COMBINED WITH TOMATOES AND MILD SPICES IN MEDITERRANEAN COUNTRIES. LOOK FOR FRESH OKRA THAT IS SOFT AND VELVETY, NOT DRY AND SHRIVELLED.

SERVES FOUR

INGREDIENTS

450g/1lb tomatoes or 400g/14oz can chopped tomatoes
450g/1lb okra
45ml/3 tbsp olive oil
2 onions, thinly sliced
10ml/2 tsp coriander seeds, crushed
3 garlic cloves, crushed
2.5ml/½ tsp sugar
finely grated rind and juice of 1 lemon
salt and ground black pepper

COOK'S TIP
When okra pods are sliced, they ooze a sticky, somewhat mucilaginous liquid which, when cooked, acts as a thickener. It gives dishes a very distinctive texture, which not everyone appreciates. If the pods are left whole, however, as here, all you get is the delicious flavour.

1 If using fresh tomatoes, cut a cross in the blossom ends, plunge them into a bowl of boiling water for 30 seconds, then refresh them in cold water. Peel off the skins and chop the tomatoes roughly.

2 Trim off any stalks from the okra and leave whole. Heat the oil in a sauté pan and fry the onions and coriander seeds for 3–4 minutes until the onions are beginning to colour.

3 Add the okra and garlic to the pan and fry for 1 minute. Gently stir in the chopped fresh or canned tomatoes. Add the sugar, which will bring out the flavour of the tomatoes. Simmer gently for about 20 minutes, until the okra is tender, stirring once or twice.

4 Stir in the lemon rind and juice, and add salt and pepper to taste, adding a little more sugar if necessary. Serve warm or cold.

Side Dishes and Salads 55

MARQUIS POTATOES

A VARIATION ON DUCHESSE POTATOES, THESE PIPED NESTS ARE FINISHED WITH A DELICIOUSLY TANGY AND BRIGHTLY COLOURED TOMATO MIXTURE SET IN THE CENTRE.

SERVES SIX

INGREDIENTS
- 900g/2lb floury potatoes
- 450g/1lb ripe tomatoes
- 15ml/1 tbsp olive oil
- 2 shallots, finely chopped
- 25g/1oz/2 tbsp butter
- 3 egg yolks
- 60ml/4 tbsp milk
- sea salt and ground black pepper
- chopped fresh parsley, to garnish

1 Peel the potatoes and cut into small chunks. Boil in lightly salted water for 20 minutes or until very tender.

2 Meanwhile, cut a cross in the base of each tomato. Blanch them in a bowl of boiling water, then refresh them by plunging them into a bowl of cold water. Drain, peel off the skins, then cut in half and scoop out the seeds. Chop the tomato flesh.

3 Heat the olive oil in a large frying pan and fry the shallots for 2 minutes, stirring continuously. Add the chopped tomatoes to the pan and fry for a further 10 minutes, stirring frequently with a wooden spoon, until the moisture has evaporated. Set aside and keep warm.

4 Drain the potatoes in a colander, then return them to the pan and allow the steam to dry off. Set aside to cool slightly.

5 Mash the potatoes with the butter, 2 of the egg yolks and the milk. Season.

6 Preheat the grill (broiler) to high. Spoon the potato into a piping (pastry) bag fitted with a medium star nozzle. Pipe six oval nests on to a greased baking sheet. Beat the remaining yolk with a little water and brush over the potato. Grill (broil) the nests until golden. Spoon the tomato mixture into the nests, sprinkle with parsley and serve.

Side Dishes and Salads

Roasted Plum Tomatoes with Garlic

THESE ARE SO SIMPLE TO PREPARE YET TASTE ABSOLUTELY WONDERFUL. USE A LARGE, SHALLOW EARTHENWARE DISH THAT WILL ALLOW THE TOMATOES TO SEAR AND CHAR IN A HOT OVEN.

SERVES FOUR

INGREDIENTS

60ml/4 tbsp extra virgin olive oil, plus extra for greasing
8 plum tomatoes
12 garlic cloves
3 bay leaves
salt and ground black pepper
45ml/3 tbsp fresh oregano leaves, to garnish

COOK'S TIPS
- Use ripe plum tomatoes for this recipe as they keep their shape and do not fall apart when roasted at such a high temperature. Leave the stalks on, if possible.
- To give the tomatoes a bit of extra zing, add a couple of dashes of hot pepper sauce to the olive oil.

1 Preheat the oven to 230°C/450°F/Gas 8. Select an ovenproof dish that will hold all the tomatoes snugly in a single layer. Grease it lightly with olive oil.

2 Cut the plum tomatoes in half lengthways. Place them in the dish, cut sides uppermost, and push the whole, unpeeled garlic cloves between them.

3 Brush the tomatoes with the oil, add the bay leaves and sprinkle black pepper over the top. Roast for about 45 minutes until the tomatoes have softened and are sizzling in the dish. They should be charred around the edges. Season with salt and a little more black pepper, if needed. Garnish with oregano and serve.

Roasted Peppers with Tomatoes

If you have time, make and dress this salad an hour or two before serving, as this will allow the juices to mingle and create the best mouthwatering Sicilian-style salad.

SERVES FOUR

INGREDIENTS

- 1 red (bell) pepper
- 1 yellow (bell) pepper
- 4 ripe plum tomatoes, sliced
- 2 canned artichokes, drained and quartered
- 4 sun-dried tomatoes in oil, drained and thinly sliced
- 15ml/1 tbsp capers, drained
- 1 garlic clove, sliced
- 1 tbsp pinenuts

For the dressing
- 15ml/1 tbsp balsamic vinegar
- 5ml/1 tsp lemon juice
- 75ml/5 tbsp extra virgin olive oil
- 4 tbsp chopped fresh mixed herbs
- salt and ground black pepper

VARIATION
The flavour of the salad can be varied by using different herbs. Rocket (arugula) will give the salad a peppery flavour.

1 Cut the peppers in half, and remove the seeds and stalks. Cut into quarters and place on a grill (broiler) pan covered with foil. Cook, skin-side up, under a grill (broiler) set on high, until the skin chars. Transfer to a bowl and cover with a plate or tuck a dishtowel around the peppers on the grill pan, to trap the steam. Leave the peppers to cool.

2 Use your fingers to peel the skin off the peppers and then cut into strips.

3 Arrange the peppers, fresh tomatoes and artichokes on a serving dish. Sprinkle over the sun-dried tomatoes, capers, garlic and pinenuts.

4 To make the dressing, put the balsamic vinegar and lemon juice in a bowl and whisk in the olive oil, then the chopped herbs. Season with salt and pepper. Pour the dressing over the salad an hour before serving. Garnish with fresh basil, if you like.

Courgettes in Tomato Sauce

This richly flavoured Mediterranean dish can be served hot or cold as a side dish. Cut the courgettes into fairly thick slices, so that they stay slightly crunchy.

SERVES FOUR

INGREDIENTS

- 15ml/1 tbsp extra virgin olive oil or sunflower oil
- 1 onion, chopped
- 1 garlic clove, chopped
- 4 courgettes (zucchini), thickly sliced
- 400g/14oz can tomatoes
- 2 tomatoes, peeled, seeded and chopped
- 5ml/1 tsp vegetable bouillon powder
- 15ml/1 tbsp tomato purée (paste)
- salt and ground black pepper

1 Heat the oil in a heavy pan, add the onion and garlic and sauté for 5 minutes or until the onion is softened, stirring occasionally. Add the courgettes and cook for a further 5 minutes, stirring occasionally.

2 Add the canned and fresh tomatoes, bouillon powder and tomato purée. Stir well, then simmer for 10–15 minutes until the sauce is thickened and the courgettes are just tender. Season to taste and serve.

Spiced Turnips with Spinach and Tomatoes

Sweet baby turnips, tender spinach and ripe tomatoes make tempting partners in this simple but very tasty eastern Mediterranean vegetable stew.

SERVES SIX

INGREDIENTS

- 450g/1lb plum tomatoes
- 2 onions
- 60ml/4 tbsp olive oil
- 450g/1lb baby turnips, peeled
- 5ml/1 tsp paprika
- 2.5ml/½ tsp sugar
- 60ml/4 tbsp chopped fresh coriander (cilantro)
- 450g/1lb fresh young spinach
- salt and ground black pepper

VARIATION

Try this with celery hearts instead of baby turnips. It is also good with fennel or drained canned artichoke hearts.

1 Plunge the tomatoes into a bowl of boiling water for 30 seconds or so, then refresh in a bowl of cold water. Drain, peel away the tomato skins and chop the flesh roughly.

2 Slice the onions. Heat the olive oil in a large frying pan or sauté pan and gently fry the onion slices for about 5 minutes until golden. Ensure that they do not blacken.

3 Add the baby turnips, tomatoes and paprika to the pan with 60ml/4 tbsp water and cook until the tomatoes are pulpy. Cover the pan with a lid and continue cooking until the baby turnips have softened.

4 Stir in the sugar and coriander, then add the spinach and a little salt and ground black pepper. Cook the mixture for a further 2–3 minutes until the spinach has wilted. The dish can be served warm or cold.

Tomato and Vegetable Bake

This dish has been made for centuries in the south of France – in the days before home kitchens had ovens, the assembled dish was carried to the baker's to make use of the heat remaining after the bread was baked.

SERVES FOUR

INGREDIENTS
- 15ml/1 tbsp olive oil, plus extra for drizzling
- 1 large onion, sliced
- 1 garlic clove, finely chopped
- 450g/1lb tomatoes
- 450g/1lb courgettes (zucchini)
- 5ml/1 tsp dried basil
- 30ml/2 tbsp freshly grated Parmesan cheese
- salt and ground black pepper

1 Preheat the oven to 180°C/350°F/Gas 4. Heat the oil in a heavy pan over a low heat and cook the onion and garlic for about 20 minutes until soft and golden.

2 Meanwhile, cut the tomatoes into 5mm/¼in thick slices. (If the tomatoes are very large, cut the slices in half.) Cut the courgettes diagonally into slices about 1cm/½in thick. When the onions are soft, spread the mixture over the base of a shallow ovenproof dish.

3 Arrange alternate rows of courgettes and tomatoes over the onion mixture and sprinkle with the basil, cheese and salt and pepper. Drizzle with olive oil, then bake for 25 minutes until the vegetables are tender. Serve the dish hot or warm.

Baked Tomatoes Provençal Style

These tomatoes, epitomizing the flavour of Provence, France, are perfect with roast meat or poultry. You can prepare them a few hours ahead, then cook them while carving the roast. They are particularly good with roast lamb or beef.

SERVES FOUR

INGREDIENTS
- 2 large tomatoes
- 45ml/3 tbsp fresh white breadcrumbs
- 2 garlic cloves, very finely chopped
- 30ml/2 tbsp chopped fresh parsley
- 30–45ml/2–3 tbsp olive oil
- salt and ground black pepper
- fresh flat leaf parsley sprigs, to garnish

VARIATIONS
- This is a very versatile recipe. Use wholemeal (whole-wheat) breadcrumbs, if you like, and try adding finely chopped hazelnuts or flaked (sliced) almonds.
- Alternatively, fry finely chopped mushrooms and garlic in a little oil, bind with breadcrumbs and use instead of the dry crumb topping.

1 Preheat the oven to 220°C/425°F/Gas 7. Cut the tomatoes in half and arrange them cut-side up on a foil-lined baking sheet.

2 In a bowl, mix together the breadcrumbs, garlic and parsley. Stir in salt and pepper to taste, then spoon the mixture over the tomato halves.

3 Drizzle the tomatoes generously with olive oil and bake them for about 8–10 minutes until lightly browned. Serve immediately, garnished with the parsley sprigs.

COOK'S TIP
If the tomato halves do not sit straight, cut a thin slice from the bases.

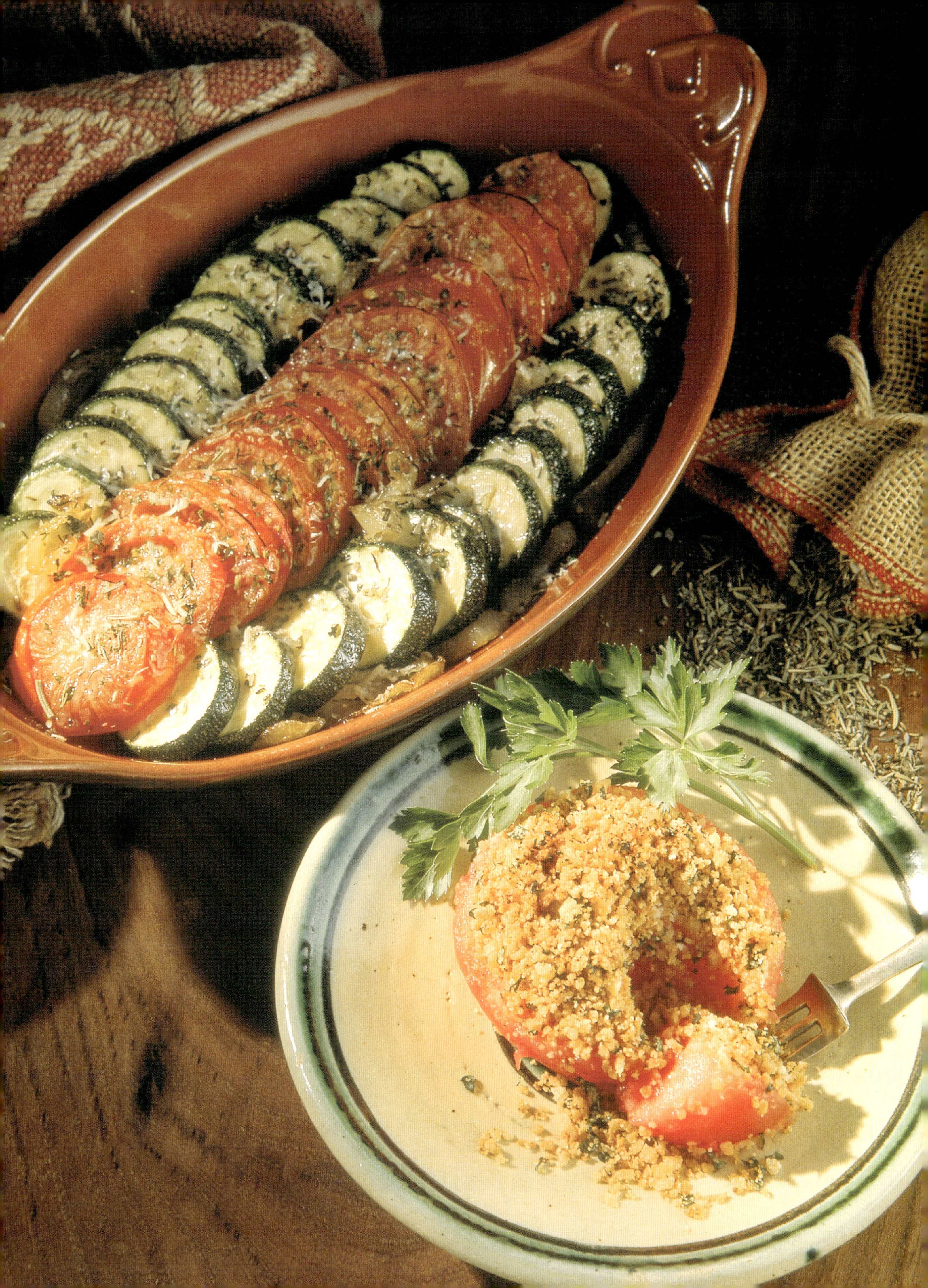

Fattoush

This is a delicious Lebanese dish, full of the flavour of fresh herbs and lemons. It makes a delicious snack or an exciting addition to a buffet table.

SERVES FOUR

INGREDIENTS
- 1 yellow or red (bell) pepper
- 1 large cucumber
- 4–5 tomatoes
- 1 bunch spring onions (scallions)
- 30ml/2 tbsp finely chopped fresh parsley
- 30ml/2 tbsp finely chopped fresh mint
- 30ml/2 tbsp finely chopped fresh coriander (cilantro)
- 2 garlic cloves, crushed
- 75ml/5 tbsp olive oil
- juice of 2 lemons
- salt and freshly ground black pepper
- 4 pitta breads

1 Slice the pepper, discarding the seeds and core, then slice or chop the flesh. Leaving the skin on the cucumber, roughly chop it. Dice the tomatoes. Place them in a large salad bowl.

2 Slice the spring onions. Add to the cucumber, tomatoes and pepper with the parsley, mint and coriander.

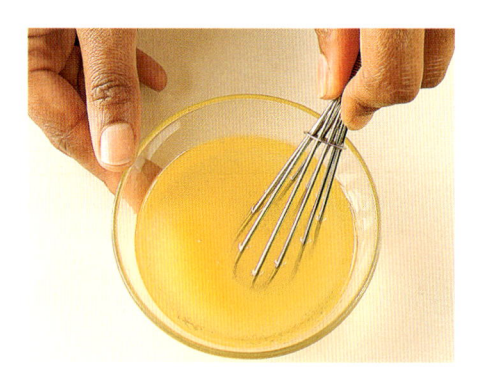

3 To make the dressing, mix the garlic with the olive oil and lemon juice. Whisk well, then season to taste.

4 Pour the dressing over the salad and toss lightly to mix.

5 Toast the pitta breads in a toaster or under a hot grill (broiler) until crisp and serve them with the salad.

COOK'S TIP
Although the recipe calls for only 30ml/2 tbsp of each of the herbs, if you have plenty to hand, you can add as much as you like to this aromatic salad.

VARIATION
If you prefer, make this salad in the traditional way. After toasting the pitta breads until crisp, crush them in your hand and then sprinkle them all over the salad before serving.

Mango, Tomato and Red Onion Salad

This salad makes an appetizing side dish. The mango has a subtle sweetness and its flavour blends well with the tomato, onion and cucumber.

SERVES FOUR

INGREDIENTS
- 1 firm mango
- 2 large tomatoes or 1 beefsteak tomato, sliced
- ½ red onion, sliced into rings
- ½ cucumber, peeled and thinly sliced
- 30ml/2 tbsp sunflower oil
- 15ml/1 tbsp lemon juice
- 1 garlic clove, crushed
- 2.5ml/½ tsp hot pepper sauce
- salt and ground black pepper
- sugar, to taste
- chopped chives, to garnish

COOK'S TIP
Choose a mango that is slightly under-ripe. The flesh should be fairly firm for this salad, but not hard.

1 Cut away two thick slices either side of the mango stone (pit) and cut into finer slices. Peel off the skin.

2 Arrange the mango, tomato, onion and cucumber slices in circles on a large serving plate.

3 Blend the oil, lemon juice, garlic, hot pepper sauce, salt and pepper in a blender or food processor, or place in a small jar and shake vigorously. Add a pinch of sugar to taste and mix again.

4 Using a teaspoon, drizzle the dressing over the salad, taking care not to disturb the slices of mango, tomato, onion and cucumber. Sprinkle with the chopped chives and serve.

64 Side Dishes and Salads

Turkish Tomato Salad

THIS CLASSIC SALAD IS A WONDERFUL COMBINATION OF TEXTURES AND FLAVOURS. THE SALTINESS OF THE CHEESE IS PERFECTLY BALANCED BY THE REFRESHING SALAD VEGETABLES.

SERVES FOUR

INGREDIENTS
- 1 cos (romaine) lettuce heart
- 1 green (bell) pepper
- 1 red (bell) pepper
- ½ cucumber
- 4 tomatoes
- 1 red onion
- 225g/8oz feta cheese, crumbled
- black olives, to garnish

For the dressing
- 45ml/3 tbsp extra virgin olive oil
- 45ml/3 tbsp lemon juice
- 1 garlic clove, crushed
- 15ml/1 tbsp chopped fresh parsley
- 15ml/1 tbsp chopped fresh mint
- salt and ground black pepper

1 Chop the lettuce into bitesize pieces. Seed the peppers, remove the cores and cut the flesh into thin strips. Chop the cucumber and slice or chop the tomatoes. Cut the onion in half, then slice finely.

2 Place the chopped lettuce, peppers, cucumber, tomatoes and onion in a large bowl. Sprinkle the feta over the top and toss together lightly.

3 To make the dressing: blend together the extra virgin olive oil, lemon juice and garlic in a small bowl or a screw-top jar. Stir in the freshly chopped parsley and mint, and season with salt and pepper to taste.

4 Pour the dressing over the salad, toss lightly with your hands until well coated, then garnish with a few black olives. Serve immediately.

Persian Salad with Tomatoes

THIS VERY SIMPLE SALAD IS ESPECIALLY GOOD SERVED WITH MEAT OR RICE DISHES – DON'T ADD THE DRESSING UNTIL JUST BEFORE YOU ARE READY TO SERVE.

SERVES FOUR

INGREDIENTS
- 4 tomatoes
- ½ cucumber
- 1 onion
- 1 cos (romaine) lettuce heart

For the dressing
- 30ml/2 tbsp olive oil
- juice of 1 lemon
- 1 garlic clove, crushed
- salt and ground black pepper

VARIATION
Use lime juice for this dressing – it will add a deliciously aromatic flavour and be slightly sweeter too.

1 Peel and seed the tomatoes if you like, then cut them into small cubes. Cube the cucumber, leaving the skin on or removing it. Finely chop the onion and tear the lettuce into pieces.

2 Place the tomatoes, cucumber, onion and lettuce in a large salad bowl and mix lightly together.

3 To make the dressing, pour the olive oil into a small bowl. Add the lemon juice, garlic and seasoning, and whisk together well. Alternatively, combine the dressing ingredients in a screw-top jar, close tightly and shake vigorously. Pour the dressing over the salad and toss lightly to mix. Sprinkle with black pepper before serving.

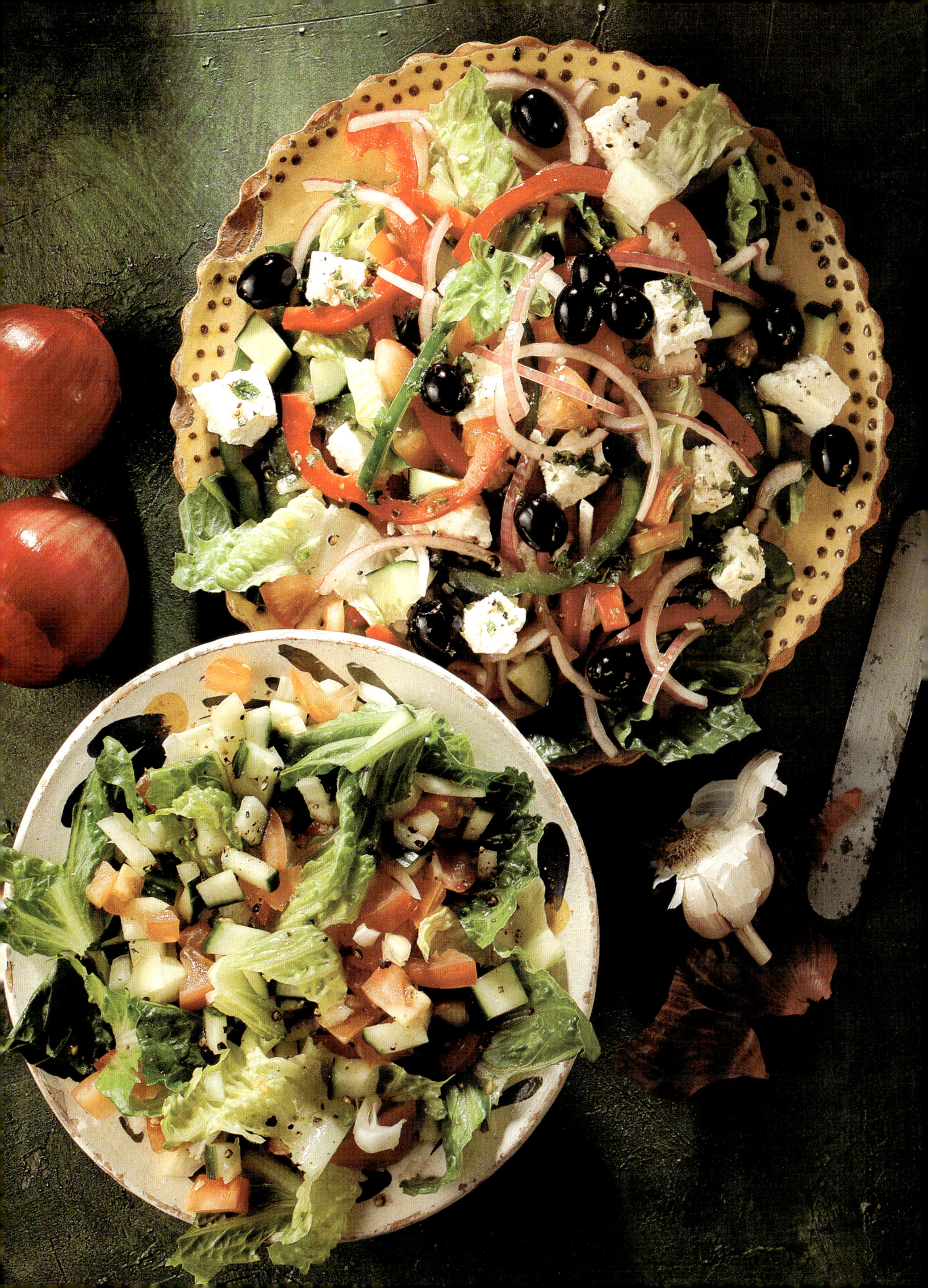

Bulgur Wheat and Cherry Tomato Salad

This appetizing salad is ideal served with fresh crusty bread and home-made chutney or pickle. It also makes a very good accompaniment to grilled meat or fish.

SERVES SIX

INGREDIENTS
- 350g/12oz/2 cups bulgur wheat
- 225g/8oz frozen broad (fava) beans
- 115g/4oz/1 cup frozen petits pois (baby peas)
- 225g/8oz cherry tomatoes, halved
- 1 sweet onion, chopped
- 1 red (bell) pepper, seeded and diced
- 50g/2oz mangetouts (snow peas), chopped
- 50g/2oz watercress or American cress
- 45ml/3 tbsp chopped fresh herbs, such as parsley, basil and thyme

For the dressing
- 75ml/5 tbsp olive oil
- 15ml/1 tbsp white wine vinegar
- 5ml/1 tsp mustard powder
- salt and ground black pepper

1 Put the bulgur wheat into a large bowl. Add enough cold water to come 2.5cm/1in above the level of the wheat. Leave to soak for approximately 30 minutes, then tip into a sieve lined with a clean dishtowel. Drain the wheat well and use the dishtowel to squeeze out any excess water.

2 Cook the broad beans and petits pois in a pan of boiling water for about 3 minutes, until tender. Drain thoroughly and mix with the prepared bulgur wheat in a bowl.

3 Add the cherry tomatoes, onion, pepper, mangetouts and watercress to the bulgur wheat mixture and mix. Combine all the ingredients for the dressing, season and stir well.

4 Add the herbs, seasoning and enough dressing to taste, tossing the ingredients together. Serve immediately or cover and chill in the refrigerator first.

AVOCADO, TOMATO AND ORANGE SALAD

THIS SALAD HAS A FEEL OF THE MEDITERRANEAN – AVOCADOS ARE GROWN IN MANY PARTS OF THE REGION AND ADD A DELICIOUS FLAVOUR AND TEXTURE TO THIS DISH. TAKE CARE TO FIND AVOCADOS THAT ARE FULLY RIPE, BUT NOT OVER-RIPE.

SERVES FOUR

INGREDIENTS
- 2 oranges
- 4 well-flavoured tomatoes
- 2 small avocados
- 60ml/4 tbsp extra virgin olive oil
- 30ml/2 tbsp lemon juice
- 15ml/1 tbsp chopped fresh parsley
- 1 small onion, sliced into rings
- salt and ground black pepper
- 25g/1oz/¼ cup flaked (sliced) almonds and olives, to garnish

COOK'S TIP
Use avocados that are just ripe for this salad. They should yield to gentle pressure. Avoid any avocados with bruised areas, or that feel very soft. Unripe avocados will ripen in 4–7 days if stored at room temperature; sooner if you have bananas in the same bowl.

1 Peel the oranges and slice into thick rounds. Plunge the tomatoes into boiling water for 30 seconds, then refresh in cold water. Peel off the skins, cut the tomatoes into quarters, remove the seeds and chop roughly.

2 Cut the avocados in half, remove the stones (pits) and carefully peel away the skin. Cut into chunks.

3 Whisk together the olive oil, lemon juice and parsley. Season with salt and pepper. Toss the avocados and tomatoes in half the dressing.

4 Arrange the sliced oranges on a plate and scatter over the onion rings. Drizzle with the rest of the dressing. Spoon the avocados, tomatoes, almonds and olives on top of the salad.

Grilled Leek and Fennel Salad with Spicy Tomato Dressing

This is an excellent salad to make in the early autumn, when young leeks are at their best and ripe tomatoes are full of flavour. Serve with good bread as an appetizer or serve to accompany simply cooked white fish for a main course.

SERVES SIX

INGREDIENTS

- 675g/1½lb leeks
- 2 large fennel bulbs
- 120ml/4fl oz/½ cup extra virgin olive oil
- 2 shallots, chopped
- 150ml/¼ pint/⅔ cup dry white wine or white vermouth
- 5ml/1 tsp fennel seeds, crushed
- 6 fresh thyme sprigs
- 2–3 bay leaves
- good pinch of dried red chilli flakes
- 350g/12oz tomatoes, peeled, seeded and diced
- 5ml/1 tsp sun-dried tomato paste (optional)
- good pinch of sugar (optional)
- 75g/3oz/¾ cup small black olives
- salt and ground black pepper

1 Cook the leeks in boiling salted water for 4–5 minutes. Use a slotted spoon to remove the leeks and place them in a colander to drain thoroughly and cool. Reserve the cooking water in the pan. Squeeze out excess water and cut the leeks into 7.5cm/3in lengths.

COOK'S TIP
When buying fennel, look for rounded bulbs; they have a better shape for this dish. The flesh should be crisp and white, with no signs of bruising. Avoid specimens with broken leaves or with brown or dried-out patches.

2 Trim the fennel bulbs, reserving any tops for the garnish, if you like, and cut the bulbs either into thin slices or into thicker wedges, according to taste.

3 Cook the fennel in the reserved cooking water for about 5 minutes, then drain thoroughly and toss with 30ml/ 2 tbsp of the olive oil. Season to taste with black pepper.

4 Heat a ridged cast-iron griddle under the grill (broiler). Arrange the leeks and fennel on the griddle and cook until tinged deep brown. Remove the vegetables from the griddle, place in a large shallow dish and set aside.

5 Place the remaining olive oil, the shallots, white wine or vermouth, crushed fennel seeds, thyme, bay leaves and chilli flakes in a large pan and bring to the boil over a medium heat. Lower the heat and simmer for 10 minutes.

6 Add the diced tomatoes and cook briskly for 5–8 minutes, or until they have reduced and the consistency has thickened.

7 Add the tomato paste, if using, and adjust the seasoning, adding a good pinch of sugar if you think the dressing needs it.

8 Pour the dressing over the leeks and fennel, toss to mix and leave to cool. The salad may be made several hours in advance and kept in the refrigerator, but bring it back to room temperature before serving.

9 When ready to serve, stir the salad then sprinkle the chopped fennel tops, if using, and black olives over the top of the dish.

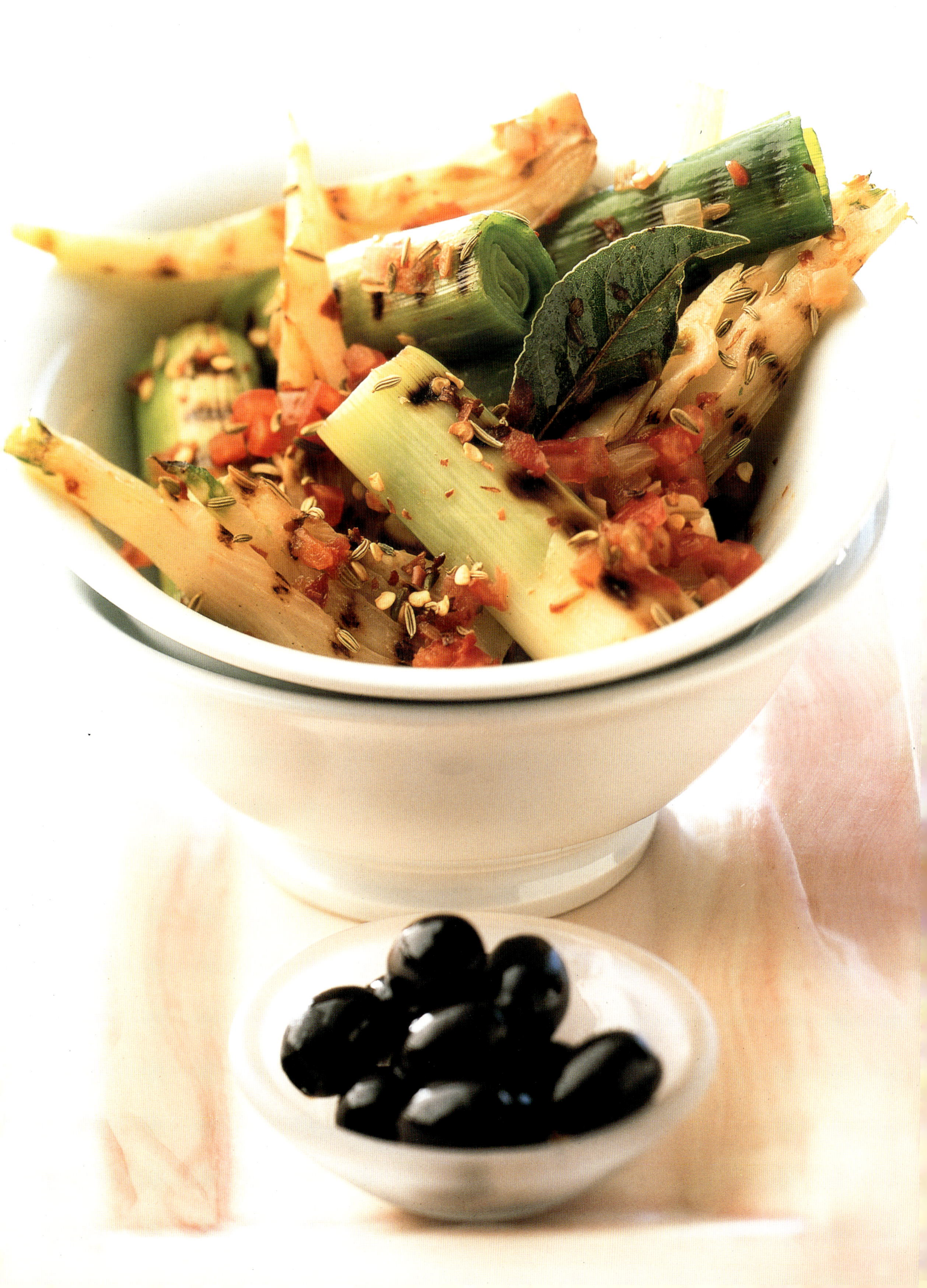

Cucumber and Tomato Salad

This salad comes from Bulgaria, where it was traditionally made with the local yogurt. It is claimed that yogurt was first made in Bulgaria.

SERVES FOUR

INGREDIENTS
- 450g/1lb firm ripe tomatoes
- ½ cucumber
- 1 onion
- 1 small fresh red or green chilli, seeded and chopped, or fresh chives, chopped into 2.5cm/1in lengths, to garnish
- crusty bread or pitta breads, to serve

For the dressing
- 60ml/4 tbsp olive or vegetable oil
- 90ml/6 tbsp thick Greek (US strained plain) yogurt
- 30ml/2 tbsp chopped fresh parsley or chives
- 2.5ml/½ tsp vinegar
- salt and ground black pepper

1 Skin the tomatoes by plunging them in boiling water for 30 seconds, then drain and plunge into cold water. Skin the tomatoes and seed and chop into even-size pieces.

2 Chop the cucumber and onion into pieces of similar size to the tomatoes and put them all in a bowl.

3 Mix all the dressing ingredients together and season to taste. Pour the dressing over the salad and toss all the ingredients together.

4 Sprinkle over black pepper and garnish with the chopped chilli or chives. Serve with chunks of crusty bread or pile into pitta pockets.

Black Olive, Tomato and Sardine Salad

The combination of ingredients in this salad — sardines, olives, tomatoes and wine vinegar — bring a real burst of flavour to a delightful light summer dish.

SERVES SIX

INGREDIENTS
- 8 large firm ripe tomatoes
- 1 large red onion
- 60ml/4 tbsp white wine vinegar
- 90ml/6 tbsp good olive oil
- 18–24 small sardines, cooked
- 75g/3oz/¾ cup pitted black olives, well drained
- salt and ground black pepper
- 45ml/3 tbsp chopped fresh parsley, to garnish

1 Slice the tomatoes into 5mm/¼in slices. Slice the onion thinly.

2 Arrange the tomatoes on individual plates, overlapping the slices, then top with the red onion.

3 Mix together the wine vinegar, olive oil and seasoning, and spoon over each plate of salad.

4 Top each salad with 3–4 sardines and a few black olives. Sprinkle the chopped parsley over the top.

COOK'S TIPS
- Use extra virgin olive oil for the dressing.
- You may not need all the vinegar as the juice from the tomatoes will contribute some acidity.

VARIATION
This recipe works equally well if the sardines are replaced with 6 shelled and halved hard-boiled eggs.

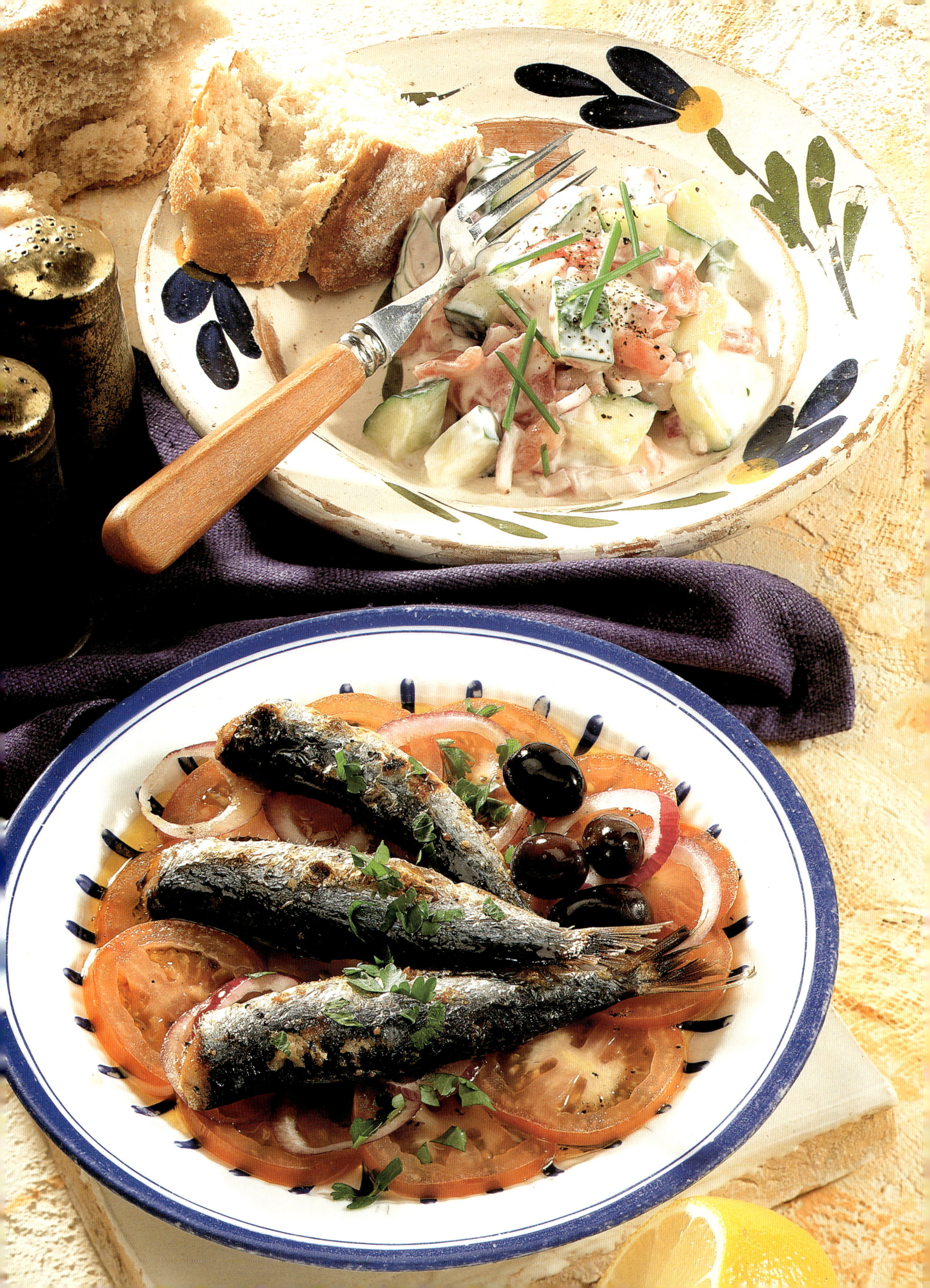

Spicy Tuna, Chickpea and Cherry Tomato Salad

A quick and easy salad using canned chickpeas and tuna with a tasty spicy tomato dressing. It would be perfect for a picnic.

SERVES SIX

INGREDIENTS

5ml/1 tsp olive oil
1 garlic clove
5ml/1 tsp ground coriander
5ml/1 tsp garam masala
5ml/1 tsp hot chilli powder
120ml/4fl oz/½ cup tomato juice
30ml/2 tbsp balsamic vinegar
dash of Tabasco sauce
½ cucumber
675g/1½lb cherry tomatoes
1 bunch radishes
1 bunch spring onions (scallions)
50g/2oz watercress or American cress
2–3 fresh parsley sprigs
1 small bunch fresh chives
2 x 400g/14oz cans chickpeas, rinsed and drained
400g/14oz can tuna in brine or water, drained and flaked
salt and ground black pepper

1 Heat the oil in a small pan. Crush the garlic in a garlic press, add it and the spices to the pan and cook gently for 1 minute, stirring constantly with a wooden spoon.

2 Stir the tomato juice, vinegar and Tabasco sauce into the oil mixture and heat until it bubbles gently. Remove the pan from the heat and set aside to cool slightly.

3 Leave the skin on the cucumber, or remove it, as you prefer. Slice the cucumber into thin rounds. If you prefer, you can slice the cucumber lengthways, take out the seeds and then slice it into rounds.

4 Halve the cherry tomatoes. Trim and slice the radishes and spring onions. Remove any tough stems from the watercress and chop it roughly.

5 Put the tomatoes and cucumber in a serving bowl. Add the radishes, spring onions and watercress to the salad bowl. Toss lightly to mix.

6 Chop the parsley finely and then bunch the chives and snip them into short sections, using kitchen scissors.

7 Stir the chickpeas, tuna and herbs into the salad. Pour the cooled tomato dressing over the salad and toss the ingredients together to mix well. Season to taste with salt and ground black pepper and serve.

Smoked Bacon and Tomato Salad with Pasta Twists

This tasty pasta salad is subtly flavoured with smoked bacon, which contrasts beautifully with the fresh flavour of the tomatoes and green beans.

SERVES FOUR

INGREDIENTS
- 350g/12oz/3 cups wholemeal (wholewheat) pasta twists
- 225g/8oz/1½ cups green beans
- 8 strips of lean smoked back bacon, rind and fat removed
- 350g/12oz cherry tomatoes, halved
- 2 bunches spring onions (scallions), chopped
- 400g/14oz can chickpeas, drained
- 90ml/6 tbsp tomato juice
- 30ml/2 tbsp balsamic vinegar
- 5ml/1 tsp ground cumin
- 5ml/1 tsp ground coriander
- 30ml/2 tbsp chopped fresh coriander (cilantro)
- salt and ground black pepper

COOK'S TIP
Always rinse canned beans and pulses before using to remove as much of the brine as possible.

1 Cook the pasta in a large pan of lightly salted, boiling water for 10–12 minutes until *al dente*. Meanwhile, trim and halve the green beans and cook them in boiling water for about 5 minutes, until tender. Drain thoroughly and keep warm.

2 Preheat the grill (broiler) to high and cook the bacon for 2–3 minutes. Using tongs, turn the bacon over and cook for 2–3 minutes on the other side, until lightly done. Dice the bacon and add to the green beans.

3 Put the tomatoes, spring onions and chickpeas in a bowl and mix together. In a small bowl, combine the tomato juice, vinegar, spices, fresh coriander and seasoning, and pour over the tomato mixture.

4 Using a sieve, or pan lid, drain the pasta thoroughly and add to the tomato mixture with the green beans and chopped bacon. Toss all the ingredients together to mix. Serve the meal warm or cold.

Roasted Cherry Tomato, Pasta and Rocket Salad

This is a good side salad to accompany flame-grilled chicken, steaks or chops. Roasted tomatoes are very juicy, with an intense, smoky-sweet flavour.

SERVES FOUR

INGREDIENTS

450g/1lb ripe baby Italian plum tomatoes, halved lengthways
75ml/5 tbsp extra virgin olive oil
2 garlic cloves, cut into thin slivers
225g/8oz/2 cups dried pasta shapes
30ml/2 tbsp balsamic vinegar
2 pieces sun-dried tomato in olive oil, drained and chopped
large pinch of granulated sugar
1 handful rocket (arugula), about 65g/2½oz
salt and ground black pepper

VARIATIONS
• If you are in a hurry and don't have time to roast the tomatoes, you can make the salad with halved raw tomatoes instead.
• If you like, add 150g/5oz mozzarella cheese, drained and diced, with the rocket in Step 4.

1 Preheat the oven to 190°C/375°F/Gas 5. Arrange the halved tomatoes cut side up in a roasting tin, drizzle 30ml/2 tbsp of the oil over them and sprinkle with the slivers of garlic and salt and pepper to taste. Roast in the oven for 20 minutes, turning once.

2 Bring a pan of lightly salted water to the boil and cook the dried pasta shapes for 10–12 minutes, or according to the instructions on the packet.

3 Put the remaining oil in a large bowl with the vinegar, sun-dried tomatoes, sugar and a little salt and pepper to taste. Stir well to mix. Drain the pasta, add it to the bowl of dressing and toss to mix. Add the roasted tomatoes and mix gently.

4 Before serving, add the rocket leaves, toss lightly and taste for seasoning. Serve either at room temperature or chilled.

Country Pasta Salad with Fresh Cherry Tomatoes

COLOURFUL, TASTY AND NUTRITIOUS, THIS IS THE IDEAL PASTA SALAD FOR A SUMMER PICNIC, AND MAKES THE MOST OF THE DELICIOUSLY SWEET CHERRY TOMATOES AVAILABLE IN THE MARKETS.

SERVES SIX

INGREDIENTS
- 300g/11oz/2¾ cups dried fusilli or other pasta shapes
- 150g/5oz green beans, cut into 5cm/2in lengths
- 1 potato, about 150g/5oz, diced into small pieces
- 200g/7oz cherry tomatoes, halved
- 2 spring onions (scallions), finely chopped, or 90g/3½oz white of leek, finely chopped
- 90g/3½oz Parmesan cheese, diced or coarsely shaved
- 6–8 pitted black olives, cut into rings
- 15–30ml/1–2 tbsp capers, to taste

For the dressing
- 90ml/6 tbsp extra virgin olive oil
- 15ml/1 tbsp balsamic vinegar
- 15ml/1 tbsp chopped fresh flat leaf parsley
- salt and ground black pepper

1 Bring a pan of lightly salted water to the boil and cook the dried fusilli for 10–12 minutes, or according to the instructions on the packet. Drain, cool and rinse under cold water, then shake the colander to remove as much water as possible. Leave to drain and dry.

2 Cook the beans and diced potato in a pan of salted boiling water for 5–6 minutes or until tender. Drain and leave the vegetables to cool.

3 Make the salad dressing. Put all the ingredients in a large serving bowl with salt and pepper to taste and whisk well to mix.

4 Add the cherry tomatoes, spring onions or leek, Parmesan, olive rings and capers to the dressing, then the cold pasta, beans and potato. Toss well to mix. Cover and leave to stand for about 30 minutes. Taste the salad and adjust the seasoning before serving.

The concentrated flavour of tomatoes adds a delicious richness to meat sauces and stews. Whether included in a main dish or as part of an accompanying sauce, their unique taste and texture is always popular. They have long been one of the most versatile ingredients to incorporate into meat dishes, as countless traditional recipes demonstrate, including Moussaka, with its deliciously creamy topping, Tagliatelle with Bolognese Sauce, and the wonderfully rich French stew, Cassoulet.

Meat and Poultry

78 Meat and Poultry

Greek Lamb Sausages WITH Tomato Sauce

The Greek name for these sausages is SOUDZOUKAKIA. *They are more like elongated meatballs than the type of sausages that we are accustomed to. Passata is sieved tomato, but home-puréed fresh tomatoes can be used, if preferred.*

SERVES FOUR TO SIX

INGREDIENTS
  50g/2oz/1 cup fresh breadcrumbs
  150ml/¼ pint/⅔ cup milk
  675g/1½lb minced (ground) lamb
  30ml/2 tbsp grated onion
  3 garlic cloves, crushed
  10ml/2 tsp ground cumin
  30ml/2 tbsp chopped fresh parsley
  plain (all-purpose) flour, for dusting
  olive oil, for frying
  600ml/1 pint/2½ cups passata
    (bottled strained tomatoes)
  5ml/1 tsp granulated sugar
  2 bay leaves
  1 small onion, peeled
  salt and ground black pepper
  flat leaf parsley, to garnish

VARIATION
• The sauce used here is based on passata, but you could substitute canned tomatoes, reduced to a purée in a blender or food processor.
• Smoked pork sausage could be used instead of the Greek sausages. Simply slice and heat in the sauce.

1 Mix together the breadcrumbs and milk. Add the lamb, onion, garlic, cumin and parsley, and season with salt and plenty of black pepper.

2 Shape the mixture with your hands into little fat sausages, each about 5cm/2in long, and roll them in flour. Heat about 60ml/4 tbsp olive oil in a large frying pan.

3 Fry the sausages for 8 minutes, turning them often. Drain. In another pan, simmer the passata, sugar, bay leaves and whole onion for 20 minutes.

4 Add the sausages to the sauce and cook for another 10 minutes. Remove the bay leaves and onion, and serve garnished with the parsley.

Lamb Burgers with Hot, Spicy Red Onion and Tomato Relish

A sharp-sweet red onion relish works well with burgers based on Middle-Eastern style lamb. Serve with pitta bread and tabbouleh or with fries and a crisp green salad.

SERVES FOUR

INGREDIENTS
- 25g/1oz/3 tbsp bulgur wheat
- 500g/1¼lb lean minced (ground) lamb
- 1 small red onion, finely chopped
- 2 garlic cloves, finely chopped
- 1 fresh green chilli, seeded and finely chopped
- 5ml/1 tsp ground toasted cumin seeds
- 2.5ml/½ tsp ground sumac
- 15g/½oz fresh flat leaf parsley, chopped
- 30ml/2 tbsp chopped fresh mint
- olive oil, for frying
- salt and ground black pepper

For the relish
- 2 red onions, cut into 5mm/¼in thick slices
- 75ml/5 tbsp extra virgin olive oil
- 2 red (bell) peppers, halved and seeded
- 350g/12oz cherry tomatoes, chopped
- 1 fresh red or green chilli, seeded and finely chopped
- 30ml/2 tbsp chopped fresh mint
- 30ml/2 tbsp chopped fresh parsley
- 15ml/1 tbsp chopped fresh oregano
- 2.5–5ml/½–1 tsp ground sumac
- 15ml/1 tbsp lemon juice
- sugar, to taste

1 Pour 150ml/¼ pint/⅔ cup hot water over the bulgur wheat in a bowl and leave to stand for 15 minutes, then tip into a sieve lined with a clean dishtowel. Drain, then squeeze out the excess moisture.

2 Place the bulgur wheat in a bowl and add the lamb, onion, garlic, chilli, cumin, sumac, parsley and mint. Mix thoroughly together by hand, then season with 5ml/1 tsp salt and plenty of ground black pepper and mix again.

3 Using your hands, form the mixture into 8 burgers and set aside while you make the relish.

4 Brush the onions with 15ml/1 tbsp of the oil and grill (broil) for about 5 minutes on each side, until well browned. Cool, then chop.

5 Grill the peppers, skin-side up, until the skin chars and blisters. Place in a bowl, cover and leave to stand for 10 minutes. Peel off the skin, dice the peppers finely and place in a bowl.

6 Add the onions to the peppers in the bowl, with the tomatoes, chilli, herbs and sumac. Stir in the remaining oil and the lemon juice. Season with salt, pepper and sugar.

7 Heat a heavy frying pan or a ridged, cast-iron grill (broiling) pan over a high heat and grease lightly with olive oil. Cook the burgers for about 5–6 minutes on each side, or until just cooked at the centre.

8 While the burgers are cooking, taste the relish and adjust the seasoning. Serve the burgers as soon as they are cooked, with the relish.

COOK'S TIP
Sumac is a sweet-sour spice made from berries. Substitute grated (shredded) lemon rind, if you prefer.

MOUSSAKA

THIS IS A TRADITIONAL EASTERN MEDITERRANEAN DISH, POPULAR IN BOTH GREECE AND TURKEY. LAYERS OF MINCED LAMB, AUBERGINES, TOMATOES AND ONIONS ARE TOPPED WITH A CREAMY YOGURT AND CHEESE SAUCE IN THIS DELICIOUS, AUTHENTIC RECIPE.

SERVES FOUR

INGREDIENTS
- 450g/1lb aubergines (eggplant)
- 150ml/¼ pint/⅔ cup olive oil
- 1 large onion, chopped
- 2–3 garlic cloves, finely chopped
- 675g/1½lb lean minced (ground) lamb
- 15ml/1 tbsp plain (all-purpose) flour
- 400g/14oz can chopped tomatoes
- 30ml/2 tbsp chopped fresh herbs
- 450g/1lb fresh tomatoes, sliced
- salt and ground black pepper

For the topping
- 300ml/½ pint/1¼ cups natural yogurt
- 2 eggs
- 25g/1oz feta cheese, crumbled
- 25g/1oz/⅓ cup freshly grated Parmesan cheese

1 Cut the aubergines into thin slices and layer them in a colander, sprinkling each layer with salt.

2 Cover the aubergines with a plate and a weight, then leave for about 30 minutes. Rinse and pat dry.

3 Heat 45ml/3 tbsp of the oil in a large, heavy pan. Fry the onion and garlic until softened, but not coloured. Add the lamb and cook over a high heat, stirring often, until browned.

4 Stir in the flour until mixed, then stir in the canned tomatoes, herbs and seasoning. Bring to the boil, reduce the heat and simmer gently for 20 minutes.

5 Meanwhile, heat a little of the remaining oil in a large frying pan. Add as many aubergine slices as can be laid in the pan, then cook until golden on both sides. Set the cooked aubergines aside. Heat more oil and continue frying the aubergines in batches, adding oil as necessary.

COOK'S TIP
Salting and drying the aubergines before frying reduces the amount of fat that they absorb and helps them to brown more quickly.

6 Preheat the oven to 180°C/350°F/Gas 4. Arrange half the aubergine slices in a large, shallow ovenproof dish, then add a layer of half the fresh tomatoes.

7 Top the slices with about half of the meat and tomato sauce mixture, then add a layer of the remaining aubergine slices, followed by the remaining tomato slices. Spread the remaining meat mixture over the aubergines and tomatoes.

8 Beat together the yogurt and eggs, then mix in the feta and Parmesan cheeses. Pour the mixture over the meat and spread it evenly.

9 Transfer the moussaka to the oven and bake for 35–40 minutes, or until golden and bubbling.

VARIATION
Use large courgettes (zucchini) instead of aubergines, if you like. Cut them diagonally into fairly thick slices.

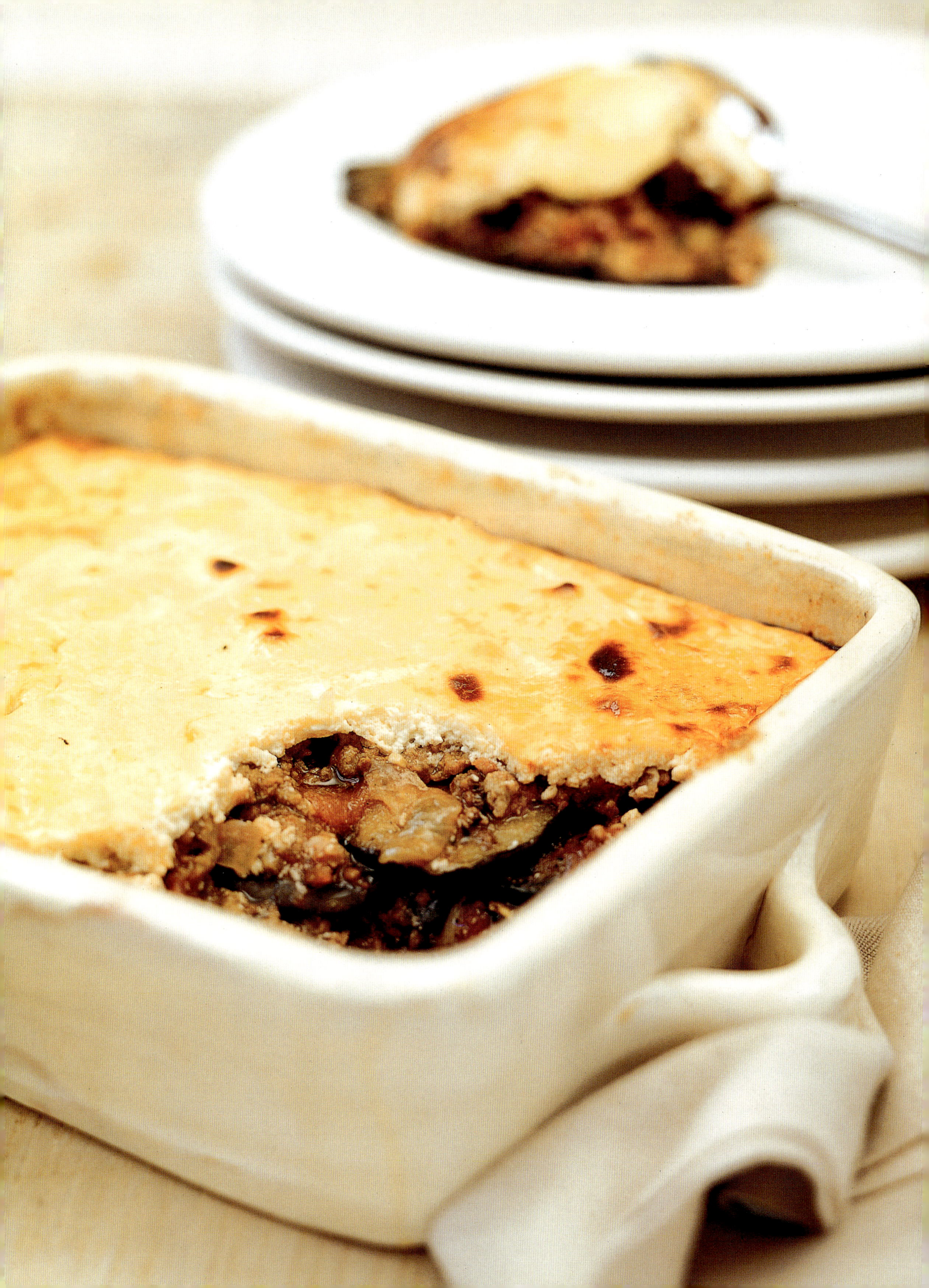

Beef and Lentil Balls with Tomato Sauce

Mixing lentils with the beef not only boosts the fibre content of these delicious and unusual meatballs but also adds to the flavour.

SERVES EIGHT

INGREDIENTS
- 15ml/1 tbsp olive oil
- 2 onions, finely chopped
- 2 celery sticks, finely chopped
- 2 large carrots, finely chopped
- 400g/14oz lean minced (ground) beef
- 200g/7oz/scant 1 cup brown lentils or green lentils
- 400g/14oz can chopped tomatoes or fresh plum tomatoes
- 30ml/2 tbsp tomato purée (paste)
- 2 bay leaves
- 300ml/½ pint/1¼ cups vegetable stock
- 175ml/6fl oz/¾ cup red wine
- 30–45ml/2–3 tbsp Worcestershire sauce
- 2 eggs
- 2 large handfuls fresh parsley, chopped
- salt and ground black pepper
- mashed potatoes and green salad, to serve

For the tomato sauce
- 4 onions, finely chopped
- 2 x 400g/14oz cans tomatoes
- 60ml/4 tbsp dry red wine
- 3 fresh dill sprigs, finely chopped

1 To make the tomato sauce, combine the onions, tomatoes and red wine in a pan. Bring to the boil, lower the heat, cover the pan and simmer for 30 minutes, stirring occasionally.

2 Purée the mixture in a blender or food processor, then return it to a clean pan and set it aside.

3 To make the meatballs, heat the oil in a large heavy pan and fry the onions, celery and carrots for 5–10 minutes, or until the onions and carrots have softened.

4 Add the minced beef and cook over a high heat, stirring frequently, until the meat is lightly browned.

5 Stir in the lentils, tomatoes, tomato purée, bay leaves, vegetable stock and wine. Bring to the boil, then simmer for 20–30 minutes until the liquid has been absorbed. Remove the bay leaves and stir in the Worcestershire sauce.

6 Remove the pan from the heat and add the eggs and parsley. Season with salt and pepper, and mix well, then leave to cool. Meanwhile, preheat the oven to 180°C/350°F/Gas 4.

7 Shape the beef mixture into neat balls, rolling them in your hands. Arrange in an ovenproof dish and bake for 25 minutes.

8 While the meatballs are baking, reheat the tomato sauce. Just before serving, stir in the chopped dill. Pour the tomato sauce over the meatballs and serve with mashed potatoes and a green salad.

COOK'S TIP
It may not be necessary to add both eggs to bind the meatballs mixture. Much will depend upon how dry the lentils are after cooking. Start with one egg. If you think the mixture needs a little more, separate the second egg and add just the yolk at first. If you miscalculate, and the mixture is too sloppy to shape, put it in the refrigerator for about 1 hour to firm up.

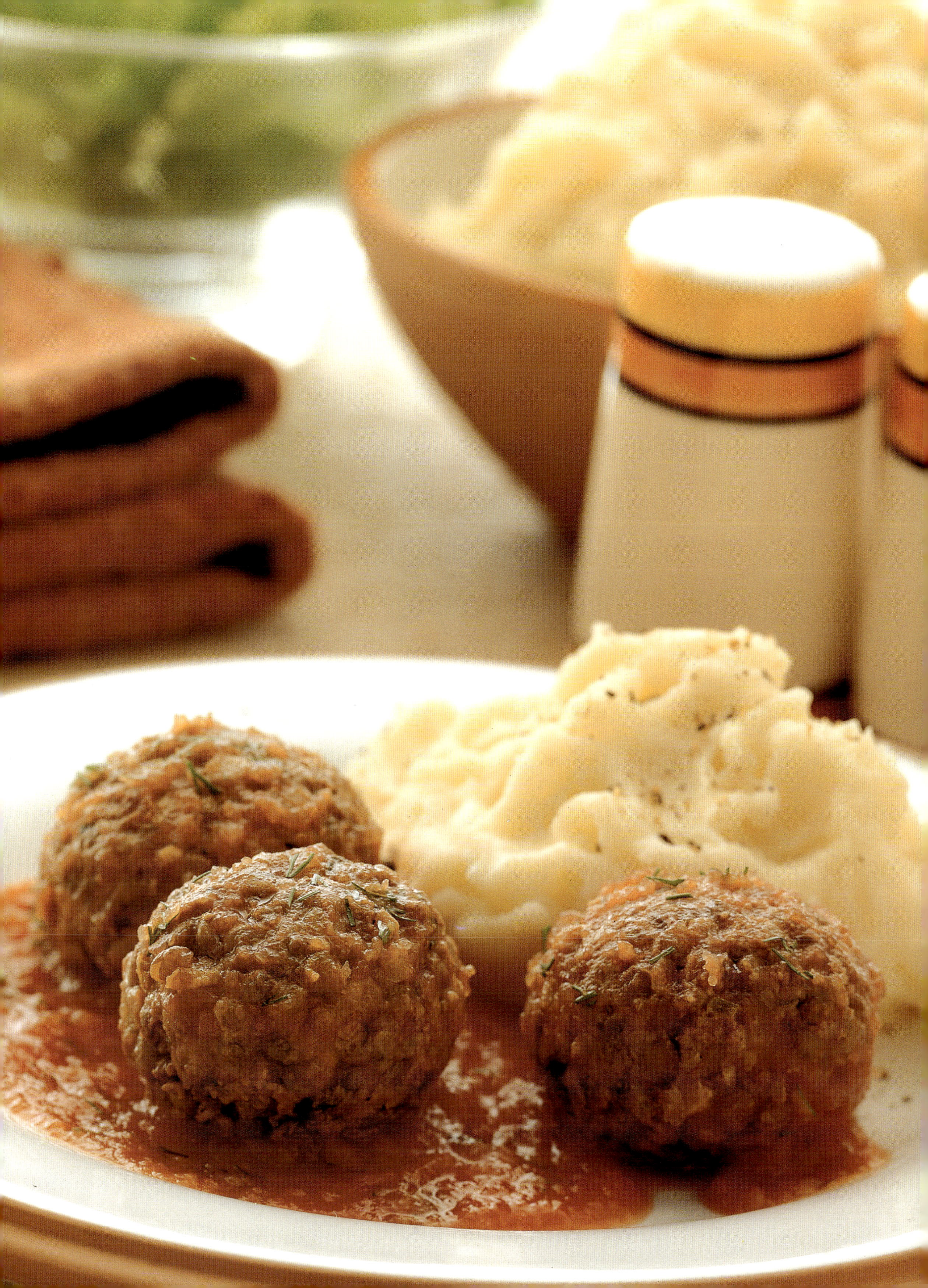

Beef Stew with Red Wine and Peas

This rich, meaty stew is perfect for a winter lunch or dinner. Serve it with boiled or mashed potatoes to soak up the deliciously tasty wine and tomato sauce.

SERVES FOUR

INGREDIENTS

- 30ml/2 tbsp plain (all-purpose) flour
- 10ml/2 tsp chopped fresh or dried thyme
- 1kg/2¼lb braising or stewing steak, cut into large cubes
- 45ml/3 tbsp olive oil
- 1 medium onion, roughly chopped
- 450ml/¾ pint/scant 2 cups passata (bottled strained tomatoes)
- 250ml/8fl oz/1 cup beef stock
- 250ml/8fl oz/1 cup red wine
- 2 garlic cloves, crushed
- 30ml/2 tbsp tomato purée (paste)
- 275g/10oz/2 cups shelled fresh peas
- 5ml/1 tsp granulated sugar
- salt and ground black pepper
- fresh thyme, to garnish

1 Preheat the oven to 160°C/325°F/Gas 3. Put the flour in a shallow dish and add the chopped fresh or dried thyme. Season with plenty of salt and pepper. Add the beef cubes and turn them in the seasoned flour until each cube is evenly coated on all sides.

2 Heat the oil in a large flameproof casserole, add the beef and brown on all sides over a medium to high heat. Remove with a slotted spoon and drain on kitchen paper.

3 Add the onion to the pan, scraping the base of the pan to mix in any residue. Cook gently for about 3 minutes, stirring frequently, until the onions have softened, then stir in the passata, stock, wine, garlic and tomato purée. Bring to the boil, stirring.

4 Return the beef to the pan and stir well to coat with the sauce. Cover and cook in the oven for 1½ hours.

5 Stir in the peas and sugar. Return the casserole to the oven and cook for 30 minutes more, or until the beef is tender. Season to taste and garnish with fresh thyme before serving.

VARIATION
Use frozen peas instead. Add them 10 minutes before the end of cooking.

Meat and Poultry 85

TAGLIATELLE WITH BOLOGNESE SAUCE

MANY PEOPLE SERVE BOLOGNESE SAUCE WITH SPAGHETTI. TO BE ABSOLUTELY CORRECT, THIS RICH ITALIAN MEAT AND TOMATO RAGU SHOULD BE SERVED WITH TAGLIATELLE.

SERVES FOUR

INGREDIENTS
- 30ml/2 tbsp olive oil
- 1 onion, finely chopped
- 1 carrot, finely chopped
- 1 celery stick, finely chopped
- 1 garlic clove, crushed
- 350g/12oz minced (ground) beef
- 150ml/¼ pint/⅔ cup red wine
- 250ml/8fl oz/1 cup milk
- 400g/14oz can chopped tomatoes
- 450g/1lb tomatoes, peeled, seeded and finely chopped
- 15ml/1 tbsp sun-dried tomato purée (paste)
- 350g/12oz dried tagliatelle
- salt and ground black pepper
- shredded fresh basil, to garnish
- grated Parmesan cheese, to serve

COOK'S TIPS
• When frying the meat, stir it constantly with a wooden spoon, making sure that any lumps are broken up.
• In winter, it is sometimes difficult to find tomatoes that are flavoursome. If the only ones you can locate taste rather dull, use an extra can of tomatoes instead.
• Don't skimp on the cooking time – it is essential for a full-flavoured Bolognese sauce. Some Italian cooks insist on cooking it for 3–4 hours, so the longer the better.

1 Heat the oil in a large pan. Add the onion, carrot, celery and garlic, and cook gently, stirring frequently, for about 10 minutes until softened.

2 Add the minced beef to the pan and cook over a medium heat until the meat changes colour.

3 Pour in the wine. Stir frequently until it has evaporated, then add the milk and continue cooking and stirring until this has evaporated, too.

4 Stir in all the tomatoes and tomato purée, and season. Simmer the sauce uncovered, over the lowest possible heat for at least 1 hour. Stir it once or twice during this time.

5 Boil the pasta for 10 minutes. Drain. Tip it into a warmed large bowl and pour over the sauce. Garnish with basil and serve with Parmesan cheese.

CASSOULET

CASSOULET IS A CLASSIC FRENCH DISH IN WHICH VARIOUS MEATS ARE BAKED SLOWLY WITH ROOT VEGETABLES AND FLAVOURSOME TOMATOES UNDER A GOLDEN CRUMB CRUST. IT IS HEARTY AND RICH.

SERVES SIX TO EIGHT

INGREDIENTS
- 675g/1½lb/3¾ cups dried haricot (navy) beans
- 900g/2lb salt belly pork
- 4 large duck breast portions
- 60ml/4 tbsp olive oil
- 2 onions, chopped
- 6 garlic cloves, crushed
- 2 bay leaves
- 1.5ml/¼ tsp ground cloves
- 60ml/4 tbsp tomato purée (paste)
- 8 good-quality sausages
- 12 large tomatoes
- 75g/3oz/¾ cup dried breadcrumbs
- salt and ground black pepper

VARIATIONS
- You can easily alter the proportions and ingredients in a cassoulet. Turnips, carrots and celeriac make suitable vegetable substitutes, while cubed lamb and goose can replace the pork and duck.
- Try topping the cassoulet with a herby breadcrumb mixture. Crumb several pieces of bread in a food processor. Stir in 10ml/2 tsp of mixed dried herbs and sprinkle over the cassoulet.

1 Put the beans in a large bowl and cover with plenty of cold water. Leave to soak overnight. Put the salt belly pork in a separate bowl of cold water and soak it overnight too.

2 Next day, drain the beans in a colander. Rinse them under cold water, drain again and put them in a pan with fresh water to cover.

3 Bring the water to the boil and boil the beans hard for 10 minutes. Drain.

4 Drain the pork, then cut it into large pieces, discarding the rind. Halve the duck breasts. Heat 30ml/2 tbsp of the oil in a frying pan and fry the pork in batches, until browned.

5 Put the beans in a large, heavy pan with the onions, garlic, bay leaves, ground cloves and tomato purée. Stir in the browned pork and just cover with water. Bring to the boil, then cover and simmer for about 1½ hours until the beans are tender.

6 Preheat the oven to 180°C/350°F/Gas 4. Heat the remaining oil in a frying pan and fry the duck breasts and sausages until browned. Cut the sausages into smaller pieces.

7 Plunge the tomatoes into boiling water for 30 seconds, then refresh in cold water. Peel off the skins and cut the tomatoes into quarters.

8 Transfer the bean mixture to a large earthenware pot or ovenproof dish and stir in the fried sausages and duck breasts and chopped tomatoes with salt and pepper to taste. Sprinkle with an even layer of breadcrumbs and bake in the oven for 45 minutes to 1 hour until the crust is golden. Serve hot.

COOK'S TIP
The best tomatoes to use for this dish are the delicious, meaty beefsteak type; if they are really large, you may only need about 8 of them. Use canned tomatoes only as a last resort.

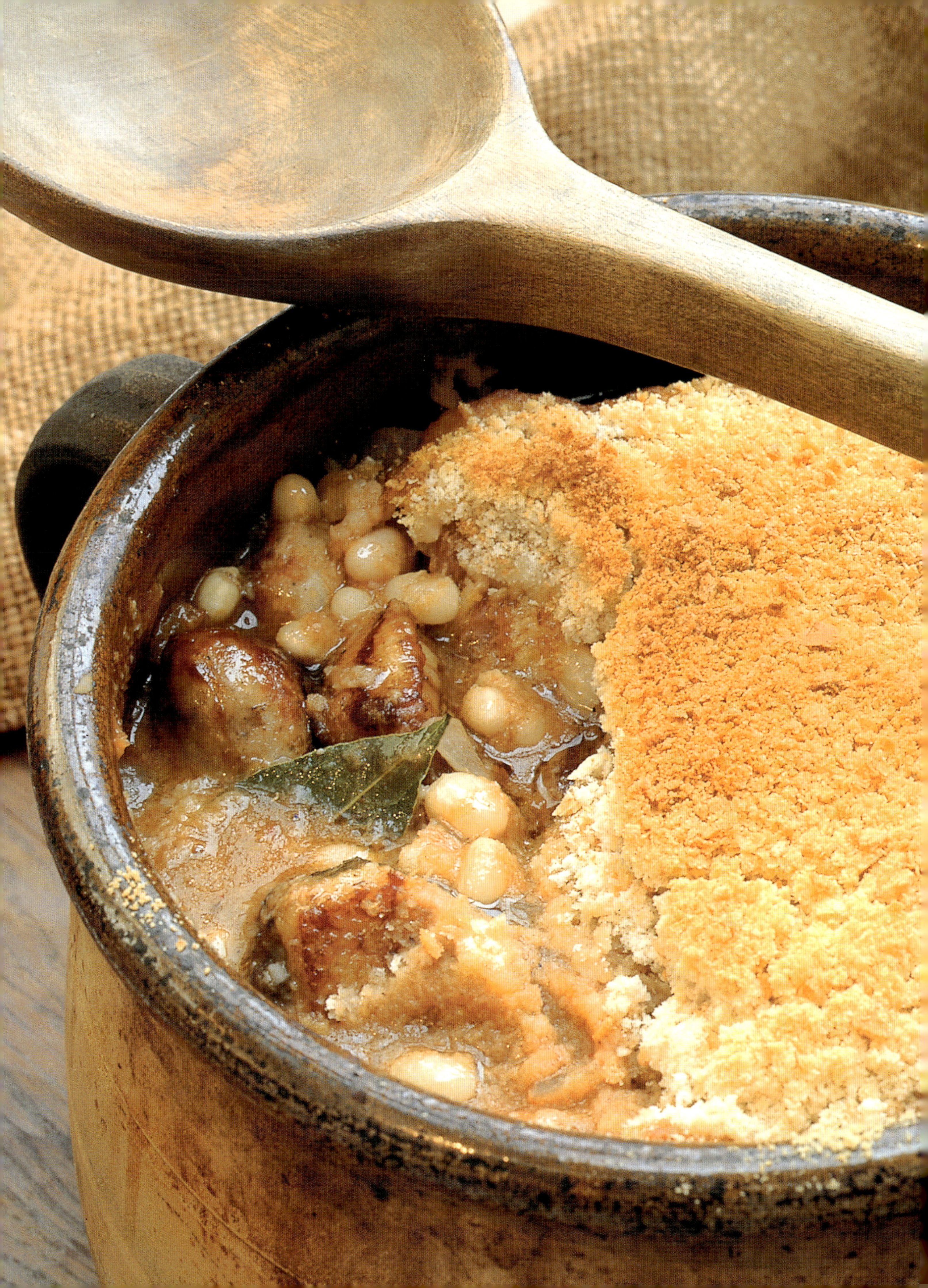

TORTIGLIONI WITH SPICY SAUSAGE SAUCE

THIS HEADY PASTA DISH BASED ON PLUM TOMATOES AND CHILLI IS NOT FOR THE FAINT-HEARTED. SERVE IT WITH A ROBUST SICILIAN RED WINE.

SERVES FOUR

INGREDIENTS

30ml/2 tbsp olive oil
1 onion, finely chopped
1 celery stick, finely chopped
2 large garlic cloves, crushed
1 fresh red chilli, seeded and chopped
450g/1lb ripe plum tomatoes, peeled and finely chopped
30ml/2 tbsp tomato purée (paste)
150ml/¼ pint/⅔ cup red wine
5ml/1 tsp granulated sugar
300g/11oz/2¾ cups dried tortiglioni, rigatoni or penne
175g/6oz spicy salami, rind removed
30ml/2 tbsp chopped fresh parsley
salt and ground black pepper
freshly grated Parmesan cheese, to serve

COOK'S TIP
Buy the salami for this dish in one piece so that you can chop it into chunks.

1 Heat the oil in a medium pan, then add the onion, celery, garlic and chilli, and cook gently, stirring frequently with a wooden spoon for about 10 minutes until the onion has softened.

2 Add the tomatoes, tomato purée, wine, sugar, and salt and pepper to taste, and bring to the boil, stirring. Lower the heat, cover and simmer gently, stirring occasionally, for about 20 minutes. Add a few spoonfuls of water occasionally if the sauce becomes too thick.

3 Meanwhile, drop the pasta into a large pan of rapidly boiling salted water and simmer, uncovered, for 10–12 minutes, until *al dente*.

4 Chop the salami into bite-size chunks and add to the sauce. Heat through, then taste for seasoning.

5 Drain the pasta, tip it into a large bowl, then pour the sauce over and toss to mix. Sprinkle over the parsley and serve with the grated Parmesan.

Hot Pepperoni Pizza

There is nothing more mouthwatering than a freshly baked pizza, especially when the topping includes tomatoes, pepperoni and red chillies.

SERVES FOUR

INGREDIENTS

- 225g/8oz/2 cups strong white bread flour
- 10ml/2 tsp easy-blend (rapid-rise) dried yeast
- 5ml/1 tsp granulated sugar
- 2.5ml/½ tsp salt
- 15ml/1 tbsp olive oil
- 175ml/6fl oz/¾ cup mixed lukewarm milk and water

For the topping
- 400g/14oz can chopped tomatoes, strained
- 2 garlic cloves, crushed
- 5ml/1 tsp dried oregano
- 225g/8oz mozzarella cheese, grated
- 2 dried red chillies, crumbled
- 225g/8oz pepperoni, sliced
- 30ml/2 tbsp drained capers
- fresh oregano, to garnish

1 Sift the flour into a bowl. Stir in the yeast, sugar and salt. Make a well in the centre. Stir the olive oil into the milk and water, then stir the mixture into the flour. Mix to a soft dough.

2 Knead the dough on a lightly floured surface for 10 minutes until it is smooth and elastic. Cover and leave in a warm place for about 30 minutes or until the dough has doubled in bulk.

3 Preheat the oven to 220°C/425°F/Gas 7. Turn the dough out on to a lightly floured surface and knead lightly for 1 minute. Divide it in half and roll each piece out to a 25cm/10in circle. Place on lightly oiled pizza trays or baking sheets. To make the topping, mix the strained tomatoes, garlic and dried oregano in a bowl.

4 Spread half the tomato mixture over each base, leaving a border around the edge. Set half the mozzarella aside. Divide the rest between the pizzas, sprinkling it over evenly. Bake for 7–10 minutes until the dough rim on each pizza is pale golden.

5 Sprinkle the crumbled chillies over the pizzas, then arrange the pepperoni slices and capers on top. Sprinkle with the remaining mozzarella. Return the pizzas to the oven and bake for 7–10 minutes more. Scatter over the fresh oregano and serve at once.

Chicken with Chorizo

The addition of chorizo sausage and sherry gives a warm, interesting flavour to this simple traditional Spanish dish. Serve with boiled potatoes or rice.

SERVES FOUR

INGREDIENTS

1 medium chicken, jointed, or 4 chicken legs, halved
30ml/2 tbsp paprika
60ml/4 tbsp olive oil
2 small onions, sliced
6 garlic cloves, thinly sliced
150g/5oz chorizo sausage, sliced
400g/14oz can chopped tomatoes
12–16 fresh bay leaves
75ml/5 tbsp medium sherry
salt and ground black pepper
potatoes or rice, to serve

COOK'S TIP

Paprika is a mild spice, made from the powdered pods of the sweet red (bell) pepper. Rose or orange in colour, it gives dishes a delicious, slightly smoky flavour, and is particularly good with pork and chicken. It is also used as a garnish.

1 Preheat the oven to 190°C/375°F/Gas 5. Coat the chicken pieces in the paprika, making sure they are evenly covered, then season with salt. Heat the olive oil in a frying pan and fry the chicken pieces until brown.

2 Transfer the chicken to an ovenproof dish. Add the onions to the pan and fry quickly. Add the garlic and sliced chorizo and fry for 2 minutes.

3 Add the tomatoes, two of the bay leaves and the sherry, and bring to the boil. Pour the sauce over the chicken and cover with a tight-fitting lid. Bake for 45 minutes.

4 Remove the lid and season to taste. Cook for a further 20 minutes until the chicken is tender and golden. Serve with potatoes or rice, garnished with the remaining bay leaves.

Varna-style Chicken

In this tasty dish, chicken portions are first fried, then smothered in a rich, herby tomato sauce and baked in the oven.

SERVES EIGHT

INGREDIENTS
- 1 chicken, about 1.8kg/4lb cut into 8 pieces, or 8 chicken portions
- 1.5ml/¼ tsp chopped fresh thyme
- 40g/1½oz/3 tbsp butter
- 45ml/3 tbsp vegetable oil
- 3–4 garlic cloves, crushed
- 2 onions, finely chopped
- salt and ground black pepper
- fresh basil and thyme leaves, to garnish
- freshly cooked rice, to serve

For the sauce
- 120ml/4fl oz/½ cup dry sherry
- 45ml/3 tbsp tomato purée (paste)
- a few fresh basil leaves
- 30ml/2 tbsp white wine vinegar
- generous pinch of granulated sugar
- 5ml/1 tsp French mustard
- 400g/14oz can chopped tomatoes
- 225g/8oz/3 cups mushrooms, sliced

COOK'S TIP
To peel a clove of garlic, place it on a board with the flat blade of a cook's knife on top of it. Press down hard on the knife blade until the garlic is sufficiently crushed to allow you to remove the skin.

1 Preheat the oven to 180°C/350°F/Gas 4. Season the chicken with salt, pepper and thyme. In a large frying pan heat the butter and oil, and cook the chicken until golden brown. Remove from the frying pan, place in an ovenproof dish and keep hot. Add the garlic and onions to the frying pan and cook for 2–3 minutes, or until soft.

2 For the sauce, mix together the sherry, tomato purée, salt and pepper, basil, vinegar and sugar. Add the mustard and tomatoes. Pour into the frying pan and bring to the boil.

3 Reduce the heat and add the mushrooms. Adjust the seasoning with more sugar or vinegar to taste.

4 Pour the tomato sauce over the chicken. Bake in the oven, covered, for 45–60 minutes, or until the chicken is cooked right through. Serve on a bed of rice, garnished with basil and thyme.

VARIATION
Replace the cultivated mushrooms with wild mushrooms, if you like.

Chicken Khoresh

This tomato-flavoured stew originates from the Middle East. It is often served on festive occasions and is traditionally believed to have been a favourite of Persian kings.

SERVES FOUR

INGREDIENTS
- 30ml/2 tbsp corn oil or extra virgin olive oil
- 1 whole chicken or 4 large chicken pieces
- 1 large onion, chopped
- 2 garlic cloves, crushed
- 400g/14oz can chopped tomatoes
- 8 fresh tomatoes, peeled, seeded and chopped
- 250ml/8fl oz/1 cup water
- 3 small aubergines (eggplant), sliced
- 3 (bell) peppers, red, green and yellow, seeded and sliced
- 30ml/2 tbsp lemon juice
- 15ml/1 tbsp ground cinnamon
- salt and ground black pepper
- boiled rice, to serve

1 Heat 15ml/1 tbsp of the oil in a large pan or flameproof casserole and fry the chicken or chicken pieces on both sides for about 8–10 minutes. Add the chopped onion and fry for a further 4–5 minutes, until the onion is golden brown. Ensure that the onion does not blacken, as this would change the flavour of the khoresh.

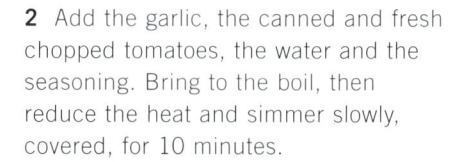

2 Add the garlic, the canned and fresh chopped tomatoes, the water and the seasoning. Bring to the boil, then reduce the heat and simmer slowly, covered, for 10 minutes.

3 Meanwhile, heat the remaining oil in a frying pan and fry the aubergines in batches until lightly golden. Transfer to a plate with a spatula or slotted spoon. Add the peppers to the pan and fry for a few minutes until they have softened slightly.

4 Arrange the aubergines over the chicken or chicken pieces and then add the peppers. Sprinkle over the lemon juice and cinnamon, then cover and continue cooking over a low heat for about 45 minutes, or until all the chicken pieces are cooked.

5 Transfer the chicken to a serving plate and spoon the aubergines and peppers around the edge. Reheat the sauce if necessary, adjust the seasoning and pour it over the chicken. Serve the khoresh with rice.

Turkey and Tomato Meatballs

A tasty change from beef or pork meatballs, these turkey meatballs are simmered with rice in a simple, but delicious, tomato sauce.

SERVES FOUR

INGREDIENTS

25g/1oz white bread, crusts removed
30ml/2 tbsp milk
1 garlic clove, crushed
2.5ml/½ tsp caraway seeds
225g/8oz minced (ground) turkey
1 egg white
350ml/12fl oz/1½ cups chicken stock
400g/14oz can tomatoes
15ml/1 tbsp tomato purée (paste)
90g/3½oz/½ cup easy-cook (converted) rice
salt and ground black pepper
15ml/1 tbsp chopped fresh basil
carrot and courgette (zucchini) ribbons, to serve

1 Cut the bread into small cubes, about 2.5cm/1in square. Put into a shallow mixing bowl. Sprinkle over the milk and leave to soak for about 5 minutes.

2 Add the garlic, caraway seeds and turkey to the soaked bread in the bowl. Season with plenty of salt and pepper. Mix together well with a spatula.

3 Whisk the egg white until stiff, then fold, half at a time, into the turkey mixture. Chill the mixture for 10 minutes in the refrigerator.

4 Put the chicken stock, canned tomatoes and tomato purée into a large, heavy pan. Quickly bring to the boil, add the rice, stir and cook briskly for about 5 minutes. Turn the heat down to a gentle simmer.

5 Shape the turkey mixture into 16 balls. Simmer them in the stock for 10 minutes, until the turkey balls and rice are cooked. Garnish with basil. Serve with carrot and courgette ribbons.

COOK'S TIP
To make carrot and courgette ribbons, cut the vegetables lengthways into thin strips using a vegetable peeler, and blanch or steam until cooked through.

Consider ripe tomatoes and fresh fish, and classic Mediterranean combinations spring to mind in which both raw ingredients are "home grown", from Black Pasta with Squid and Tomato Sauce to Baked Cod with Tomatoes and Peppers or Fresh Tuna and Tomato Stew. These tasty partners aren't unique to Europe — think spicy and aromatic, and be inspired by several mouthwatering dishes from Mexico, such as Chargrilled Swordfish with Spicy Tomato and Lime Sauce or Red Snapper Burritos with Chilli and Cheese.

Fish and Shellfish

Roasted Cod with Fresh Tomato Sauce

Really fresh cod has a sweet, delicate flavour and a pure white flaky flesh. Served with an aromatic tomato sauce, it makes a delicious meal.

SERVES FOUR

INGREDIENTS

- 350g/12oz ripe plum tomatoes
- 75ml/5 tbsp olive oil
- 2.5ml/½ tsp sugar
- 2 strips of pared orange rind
- 1 fresh thyme sprig
- 6 fresh basil leaves
- 900g/2lb fresh cod fillet, skin on
- salt and ground black pepper
- steamed green beans, to serve

COOK'S TIP

Cod is becoming increasingly rare and expensive. You can substitute any firm white fish fillets in this dish. Try haddock, pollock, or that excellent and underrated fish, coley. When raw, coley flesh looks grey, but it turns white on cooking.

1 Preheat the oven to 230°C/450°F/Gas 8. Roughly chop the tomatoes.

2 Heat 15ml/1 tbsp of the olive oil in a heavy pan, add the tomatoes, sugar, orange rind, thyme and basil, and simmer for 5 minutes until the tomatoes are soft.

3 Press the tomato mixture through a fine sieve, discarding the solids that remain in the sieve. Pour into a small pan and heat gently.

4 Scale the cod fillet and cut on the diagonal into 4 pieces. Season well.

5 Heat the remaining oil in a heavy frying pan and fry the cod, skin-side down, until the skin is crisp. Place the fish on a greased baking sheet, skin-side up, and roast in the oven for 8–10 minutes until the fish is cooked through. Serve the fish on the steamed green beans with the tomato sauce.

Baked Cod with Tomatoes and Peppers

The wonderful sun-drenched flavours of the Mediterranean are brought together in this appetizing, potato-topped bake. Red and yellow peppers add colour to the dish.

SERVES FOUR

INGREDIENTS

- 450g/1lb potatoes, peeled and thinly sliced
- 30ml/2 tbsp olive oil
- 1 red onion, chopped
- 1 garlic clove, crushed
- 1 red (bell) pepper, seeded and diced
- 1 yellow (bell) pepper, seeded and diced
- 225g/8oz/3 cups mushrooms, sliced
- 400g/14oz can chopped tomatoes
- 225g/8oz fresh tomatoes, chopped
- 150ml/¼ pint/⅔ cup dry white wine
- 450g/1lb skinless, boneless cod fillet, cut into 2cm/¾in cubes
- 50g/2oz/½ cup pitted black olives, chopped
- 15ml/1 tbsp chopped fresh basil
- 15ml/1 tbsp chopped fresh oregano
- salt and ground black pepper
- fresh oregano sprigs, to garnish
- cooked courgettes (zucchini), to serve

1 Preheat the oven to 200°C/400°F/Gas 6. Bring a large pan of lightly salted water to the boil. Add the potato slices and cook for 4 minutes. Tip into a colander, drain thoroughly, then put the potato slices into a bowl. Add 15ml/1 tbsp of the olive oil and toss gently to coat. Set aside.

2 Heat the remaining olive oil in a large pan, add the chopped onion, crushed garlic and red and yellow peppers, and cook for 5 minutes, stirring occasionally.

3 Stir in the mushrooms, tomatoes and wine, bring to the boil and boil rapidly for a few minutes to reduce.

4 Stir the fish cubes, olives and herbs into the tomato mixture, with salt and a generous grinding of black pepper. Stir well to combine.

5 Spoon the mixture into a lightly greased ovenproof dish and arrange the potato slices over the top, covering the fish mixture completely. Bake, uncovered, for about 45 minutes until the fish is cooked and tender and the potato topping is browned. Garnish with oregano and serve with courgettes.

Mexican-style Salt Cod

This traditional recipe is milder than the similar Spanish dish, Bacaldo a la Vizcaina, but is just as full of tomatoes. It is eaten on Christmas Eve throughout Mexico.

SERVES SIX

INGREDIENTS
- 450g/1lb dried salt cod
- 105ml/7 tbsp extra virgin olive oil
- 1 onion, halved and thinly sliced
- 4 garlic cloves, crushed
- 2 x 400g/14oz can chopped tomatoes
- 450g/½ lb fresh tomatoes, chopped
- 75g/3oz/¾ cup flaked (sliced) almonds
- 75g/3oz/½ cup pickled chilli slices
- 115g/4oz/1 cup green olives stuffed with pimiento
- small bunch of fresh parsley, finely chopped
- salt and ground black pepper
- fresh flat leaf parsley, to garnish
- crusty bread, to serve

1 Put the cod in a large bowl and pour over enough cold water to cover. Soak for 24 hours, changing the water at least 5 times during this period.

2 Drain the cod and remove the skin. Shred the flesh finely using two forks, and put it into a bowl. Set it aside.

3 Heat half the oil in a large frying pan. Add the onion slices and fry over a medium heat, stirring often with a wooden spoon, until the onion has softened and is translucent. Do not let the onion slices burn.

4 Remove the onion from the pan and set aside. Make sure you transfer the oil with the onion as it is an important flavouring in this dish and must not be discarded.

5 Add the remaining olive oil to the frying pan. When it is hot but not smoking, add the crushed garlic and fry gently for 2 minutes, stirring constantly with the wooden spoon.

6 Add the tomatoes and their juice to the pan and stir to mix. Cook over a medium–high heat for about 20 minutes, stirring occasionally with the wooden spoon, until the mixture has reduced and thickened. Towards the end of the cooking time, stir the sauce more frequently to make sure it does not stick on the base of the pan.

7 Meanwhile, spread out the flaked almonds in a single layer in a large heavy frying pan. Toast them over a medium heat for a few minutes, shaking the pan lightly throughout the process so that they turn golden brown all over. Do not let them burn.

8 Add the chilli slices and stuffed olives to the toasted almonds.

9 Stir in the shredded fish, mixing it in thoroughly, and cook for 20 minutes more, stirring occasionally, until the mixture is almost dry.

10 Season to taste, add the parsley and cook for a further 2–3 minutes. Garnish with parsley leaves and serve in heated bowls, with crusty bread.

COOK'S TIPS
- Salt cod is available in specialist fishmongers, Spanish delicatessens and West Indian stores.
- Any leftovers can be used to fill burritos or empanadas.

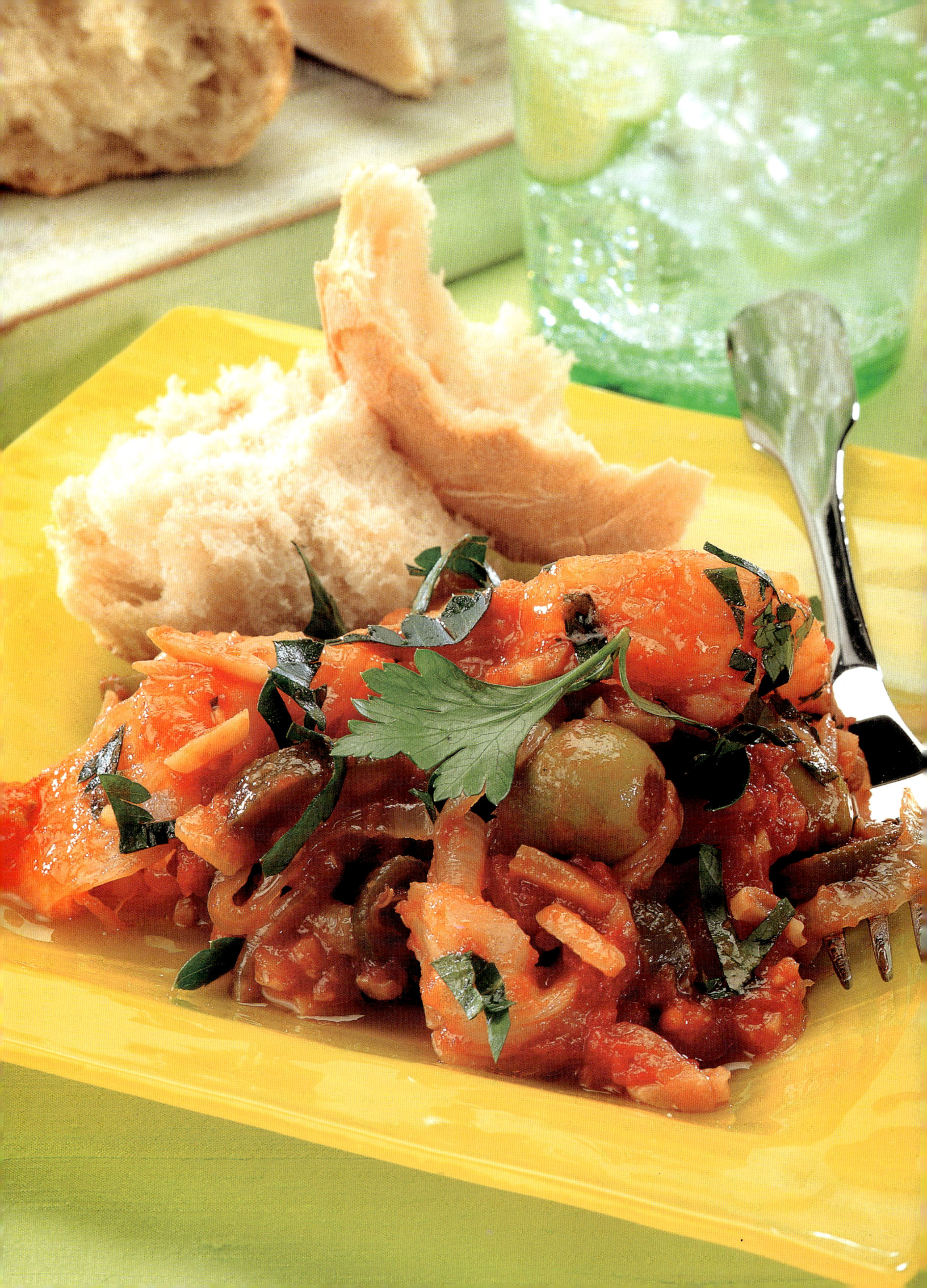

Chargrilled Swordfish WITH Spicy Tomato AND Lime Sauce

SWORDFISH IS A PRIME CANDIDATE FOR THE BARBECUE, AS LONG AS IT IS NOT OVERCOOKED. IT TASTES WONDERFUL WITH A SPICY TOMATO SAUCE WHOSE FIRE IS TEMPERED WITH CRÈME FRAÎCHE.

SERVES FOUR

INGREDIENTS
- 2 fresh chillies
- 4 tomatoes
- 45ml/3 tbsp olive oil
- grated rind and juice of 1 lime
- 4 swordfish steaks, about 225g/8oz each
- 2.5ml/½ tsp salt
- 2.5ml/½ tsp ground black pepper
- 175ml/6fl oz/¾ cup crème fraîche
- fresh flat leaf parsley, to garnish
- chargrilled vegetables, to serve

1 Roast the chillies in a dry griddle pan until the skins are blistered. Put in a plastic bag and tie the top. Set aside for 20 minutes, then peel off the skins. Cut off the stalks, then slit the chillies, take out the seeds and slice the flesh.

2 Cut a cross in the base of each tomato. Place them in a heatproof bowl and pour over boiling water to cover. After 30 seconds, lift the tomatoes out on a slotted spoon and plunge them into a bowl of cold water. Drain. The skins will have begun to peel back from the crosses.

3 Remove all the skin from the tomatoes, then cut them in half and squeeze out the seeds. Using a serrated knife, chop the tomato flesh into 1cm/½in pieces.

4 Heat 15ml/1 tbsp of the oil in a small pan and add the strips of chilli, with the lime rind and juice. Cook for 2–3 minutes, then stir in the tomatoes. Cook for 10 minutes, stirring the mixture occasionally, until the tomato is soft and pulpy.

5 Brush the swordfish steaks with the remaining olive oil and season them well. Barbecue or grill (broil) for 3–4 minutes or until just cooked, turning once. Meanwhile, stir the crème fraîche into the sauce, heat it through gently and pour over the swordfish steaks. Serve garnished with parsley and with chargrilled vegetables.

CEVICHE

THIS FAMOUS DISH IS PARTICULARLY POPULAR ALONG MEXICO'S WESTERN SEABOARD, IN PLACES SUCH AS ACAPULCO. IT CONSISTS OF VERY FRESH RAW SHELLFISH, "COOKED" BY THE ACTION OF LIME JUICE.

SERVES SIX

INGREDIENTS
- 200g/7oz raw peeled prawns (shrimp)
- 200g/7oz shelled scallops
- 200g/7oz squid, cleaned and cut into serving pieces
- 7 limes
- 12 plum tomatoes
- 1 small onion
- 1 ripe avocado
- 20ml/4 tsp chopped fresh oregano, or 10ml/2 tsp dried oregano
- 5ml/1 tsp salt
- ground black pepper
- fresh oregano sprigs, to garnish
- crusty bread and lime wedges, to serve (optional)

1 Spread out the shellfish in a non-metallic dish. Squeeze 6 limes and pour the juice over. Cover and chill for 8 hours or overnight.

2 Drain the shellfish in a colander to remove the excess lime juice, then pat it dry with kitchen paper. Place the shellfish in a bowl.

3 Cut the tomatoes in half, squeeze out the seeds, then dice the flesh. Cut the onion in half, then slice it thinly. Cut the avocado in half lengthways, remove the stone (pit) and peel, then cut the flesh into 1cm/½in dice.

4 Add the tomatoes, onion and avocado to the shellfish with the oregano and seasoning. Squeeze the remaining lime and pour over the juice. Garnish with oregano and serve, with crusty bread and lime wedges, if you like.

Red Snapper Burritos with Chilli and Cheese

Fish makes a great filling for a tortilla, especially when it is succulent red snapper mixed with rice, chilli and tomatoes.

SERVES EIGHT

INGREDIENTS

- 3 red snapper or any white fish fillets
- 90g/3½oz/½ cup long grain white rice
- 30ml/2 tbsp vegetable oil
- 1 small onion, finely chopped
- 5ml/1 tsp ground achiote seed
- 2.5ml/½ tsp chilli powder
- 200g/7oz can chopped tomatoes
- 75g/3oz/¾ cup flaked (sliced) almonds
- 150g/5oz/1¼ cups grated Monterey Jack or mild Cheddar cheese
- 8 x 20cm/8in wheat flour tortillas

1 Grill (broil) the fish on an oiled rack for about 5 minutes, turning once. When cool, remove the skin and flake the fish into a bowl. Set it aside. Meanwhile, put the rice in a pan, pour over cold water, cover and bring to the boil. Drain, rinse and drain again.

2 Heat the oil and fry the onion until soft. Stir in the ground achiote and the chilli, and cook for 5 minutes.

3 Add the rice, stir to coat all the grains in the flavoured oil, then stir in the tomatoes, flaked fish and almonds. Cook over a medium heat until the juice is absorbed and the rice is tender. Stir in the cheese and remove from the heat. Warm the tortillas.

4 Spread out the tortillas and divide the filling among them. Shape each burrito by folding the sides of the tortilla over the filling, then bringing the bottom up and the top down to form a neat parcel. Secure each burrito with a cocktail stick or toothpick until ready to serve.

Fresh Tuna and Tomato Stew

A deliciously simple Italian recipe that relies on good basic ingredients: fresh fish, tomatoes and herbs. For an authentic flavour, serve with polenta or pasta.

SERVES FOUR

INGREDIENTS

- 12 baby (pearl) onions, peeled
- 900g/2lb ripe tomatoes
- 675g/1½lb tuna
- 45ml/3 tbsp olive oil
- 2 garlic cloves, crushed
- 45ml/3 tbsp chopped fresh herbs
- 2 bay leaves
- 2.5ml/½ tsp caster (superfine) sugar
- 30ml/2 tbsp sun-dried tomato purée (paste)
- 150ml/¼ pint/⅔ cup dry white wine
- salt and ground black pepper
- baby courgettes (zucchini) and fresh herbs, to garnish

VARIATION

Two large mackerel make a more readily available alternative to the tuna. Simply lay the whole fish over the sauce and cook, covered with a lid, until the mackerel is cooked through.

1 Leave the onions whole and cook in a pan of boiling water for 4–5 minutes until softened. Drain. Plunge the tomatoes into boiling water for 30 seconds, then refresh in cold water. Peel off the skins and chop roughly.

2 Cut the tuna into 2.5cm/1in chunks. Heat the oil in a large frying or sauté pan and quickly fry the tuna until the surface has browned. Lift the chunks out of the pan and drain.

3 Stir in the onions, garlic, tomatoes, chopped herbs, bay leaves, sugar, tomato purée and wine, and bring to the boil, breaking up the tomatoes with a wooden spoon.

4 Reduce the heat and simmer the sauce gently for 5 minutes. Return the fish to the pan and cook for a further 5 minutes. Season, and serve hot, garnished with baby courgettes and fresh herbs.

BRODETTO

This robust fish and tomato stew comes from Italy. There are many versions, but all require flavoursome sun-ripened tomatoes and a good fish stock. Make sure you buy some of the fish whole so that you can simply simmer them, remove the cooked flesh and strain the deliciously flavoured juices to make the stock.

SERVES FOUR TO FIVE

INGREDIENTS

- 900g/2lb mixture of fish fillets or steaks, such as monkfish, cod, haddock, halibut or hake
- 900g/2lb mixture of conger eel, red or grey mullet, snapper or small white fish, prepared according to type
- 1 onion, halved
- 1 celery stick, roughly chopped
- 225g/8oz squid
- 225g/8oz fresh mussels
- 675g/1½lb ripe tomatoes
- 60ml/4 tbsp olive oil
- 1 large onion, thinly sliced
- 3 garlic cloves, crushed
- 5ml/1 tsp saffron threads
- 150ml/¼ pint/⅔ cup dry white wine
- 90ml/6 tbsp chopped fresh parsley
- salt and ground black pepper
- croûtons, to serve

1 Remove any skin and bones from the fish fillets or steaks, cut the fish into large pieces and reserve. Place the bones in a pan with all the remaining fish.

2 Add the halved onion and the celery and just cover with water. Bring almost to the boil, then reduce the heat and simmer gently for about 30 minutes. Lift out the fish and remove the flesh from the bones. Strain the stock.

3 To prepare the squid, twist the head and tentacles away from the body. Cut the head from the tentacles. Discard the body contents and peel away the mottled skin. Wash the tentacles and bodies and dry on kitchen paper.

4 Scrub the mussels, discarding any that are damaged or open ones that do not close when sharply tapped.

5 Plunge the tomatoes into boiling water for 30 seconds, then refresh in cold water. Peel off the skins and chop the flesh roughly.

6 Heat the oil in a large sauté pan. Add the sliced onion and the garlic, and fry gently for 3 minutes. Add the squid and the uncooked white fish, which you reserved earlier, and fry quickly on all sides. Remove the fish from the pan using a slotted spoon.

7 Add 475ml/16fl oz/2 cups strained reserved fish stock, the saffron and tomatoes to the pan. Pour in the wine. Bring to the boil, then reduce the heat and simmer for about 5 minutes. Add the mussels, cover, and cook for 3–4 minutes until the mussels have opened. Discard any mussels that remain closed.

8 Season the sauce with salt and pepper and put all the fish in the pan. Cook gently for 5 minutes. Sprinkle with the parsley and serve with the croûtons.

Fish Boulettes on Hot Tomato Sauce

This is an unusual and tasty dish that needs scarcely any preparation and leaves very few dishes to wash, as it is all cooked in one pan. It serves four people as a main course, but also makes a great appetizer for eight.

SERVES FOUR TO EIGHT

INGREDIENTS
  675g/1½lb white fish fillets
  pinch of saffron threads
  ½ bunch fresh flat leaf parsley
  1 egg
  25g/1oz/½ cup fresh white
    breadcrumbs
  25ml/1½ tbsp olive oil
  15ml/1 tbsp lemon juice
  salt and ground black pepper
  fresh flat leaf parsley and lemon
    wedges, to garnish
For the sauce
  1 onion, very finely chopped
  2 garlic cloves, crushed
  6 tomatoes, peeled and chopped
  1 fresh green or red chilli, seeded
    and finely sliced
  90ml/6 tbsp olive oil
  150ml/¼ pint/⅔ cup water
  15ml/1 tbsp lemon juice

1 Skin the fish, cut it into large chunks and place in a blender. Dissolve the saffron in 30ml/2 tbsp boiling water and pour into the blender with the parsley, egg, breadcrumbs, olive oil and lemon juice. Season well with salt and ground black pepper and process for 10–20 seconds until the fish is finely chopped and all the ingredients are combined.

2 Mould the mixture into small balls about the size of walnuts and place them in a single layer on a plate. Place in the refrigerator until ready to cook.

3 To make the sauce, place the onion, garlic, tomatoes, chilli, olive oil and water in a pan. Bring to the boil and then lower the heat and simmer, partially covered, for 10–15 minutes until the sauce is slightly reduced. Stir occasionally to prevent the mixture from sticking.

4 Stir in the lemon juice, then place the fish balls in the simmering sauce. Cover and simmer very gently for 12–15 minutes until the fish balls are cooked through, turning them over occasionally.

5 Serve the fish balls and sauce immediately from the pan, garnished with fresh flat leaf parsley and lemon wedges.

Mediterranean Fish Cutlets with Aniseed Tomato Sauce

This delicious dish is perfect for a dinner party, as the white flesh of the fish contrasts with the striking red of the sauce. The pastis in the sauce adds a surprise to the range of flavours, and will give your guests a meal to remember.

SERVES FOUR

INGREDIENTS
- 4 white fish cutlets, about 150g/5oz each
- 150ml/¼ pint/⅔ cup fish stock and/or dry white wine, for poaching
- 1 bay leaf
- a few black peppercorns
- a strip of pared lemon rind
- fresh parsley and lemon wedges, to garnish

For the tomato sauce
- 400g/14oz can chopped tomatoes
- 1 garlic clove
- 15ml/1 tbsp sun-dried tomato purée (paste)
- 15ml/1 tbsp pastis or other aniseed (anise seed) flavoured liqueur
- 15ml/1 tbsp drained capers
- 12–16 pitted black olives
- salt and ground black pepper

1 Make the sauce. Heat the chopped tomatoes in a pan with the whole garlic clove, over a medium heat. Stir in the sun-dried tomato purée.

2 Measure the pastis or other liqueur into the pan, then add the capers and olives. Season with salt and black pepper. Heat all the ingredients together for 5 minutes, stirring occasionally, to blend the flavours.

3 Place the fish in a frying pan, pour over the stock and/or wine and add the flavourings. Cover and simmer for 10 minutes or until the fish flakes easily.

4 Using a slotted spoon, transfer the fish to a heated dish. Strain the stock into the sauce and boil to reduce slightly. Season the sauce, pour it over the fish and serve immediately, with parsley and lemon wedges.

Monkfish with Tomatoes

Monkfish, also known as angler fish, was once scorned by fishermen because of its huge, ugly head, yet now it is prized for its rich, meaty texture.

SERVES FOUR

INGREDIENTS

- 800g/1¾lb monkfish tail, skinned and filleted
- plain (all-purpose) flour, for coating
- 45–60ml/3–4 tbsp olive oil or sunflower oil
- 120ml/4fl oz/½ cup dry white wine or fish stock
- 8 ripe tomatoes, peeled, seeded and chopped
- 2.5ml/½ tsp dried thyme
- 16 black olives, pitted
- 15-30ml/1–2 tbsp capers, rinsed
- 15ml/1 tbsp chopped fresh basil
- salt and ground black pepper
- pine nuts, to garnish

COOK'S TIP

The monkfish slices should only have a light dusting of seasoned flour. Drop each slice in turn into the flour, turn it until coated on all sides, then lightly jiggle it in your hand, holding the fingers slightly apart, until all the excess flour drops off. Alternatively, put the seasoned flour in a stout plastic bag, add the slices and shake gently to coat.

1 Using a thin, sharp knife, remove any pinkish membrane from the monkfish tail. Holding the knife at an angle, cut the fillets diagonally into 12 slices.

VARIATION

If monkfish is not available, try substituting any white fish, such as cod.

2 Season the flour and coat the fish in the mixture. Put a heavy frying pan on high heat and add the oil to coat. Add the monkfish slices and reduce the heat to medium–high. Cook the monkfish for 2 minutes on each side until the surface is lightly browned and the flesh is opaque. Transfer to a warmed plate while you make the sauce.

3 Add the wine or fish stock to the pan and boil for 1–2 minutes, stirring constantly. Add the tomatoes and thyme, and cook for 2 minutes, then stir in the olives, capers and basil, and cook for a further minute to heat through. Arrange three pieces of fish on each of 4 warmed plates. Spoon over the sauce and garnish with pine nuts.

Caribbean Fish Steaks

WEST INDIAN COOKS LOVE SPICES, AND USE THEM TO GOOD EFFECT. THIS QUICK AND EASY RECIPE IS A TYPICAL EXAMPLE OF HOW CHILLIES, CAYENNE AND ALLSPICE CAN BE USED WITH LIME TO ADD AN EXOTIC ACCENT TO A TOMATO SAUCE FOR FISH.

SERVES FOUR

INGREDIENTS
- 45ml/3 tbsp sunflower oil
- 6 shallots
- 1 garlic clove
- 1 fresh green chilli, seeded and finely chopped
- 400g/14oz can chopped tomatoes
- 2 bay leaves
- 1.5ml/¼ tsp cayenne pepper
- 5ml/1 tsp ground allspice
- juice of 2 limes
- 4 cod steaks
- 5ml/1 tsp muscovado (molasses) sugar
- 10ml/2 tsp angostura bitters
- salt

VARIATION
This unusual and exotic sauce is also good over grilled (broiled) pork chops.

1 Slowly heat the oil in a frying pan. Finely chop the shallots and add them to the frying pan. Cook for 5 minutes until soft. Crush a peeled garlic clove into the frying pan and add the chilli. Cook for a further 2 minutes, then stir in the tomatoes, bay leaves, cayenne pepper, allspice and lime juice, with a little salt to taste.

2 Cook gently for 15 minutes, then add the cod steaks and baste with the tomato sauce. Cover and cook for 10 minutes. Transfer the steaks to a warmed dish and keep hot while you prepare the sauce. Stir the sugar and angostura bitters into the sauce, simmer for 2 minutes, then pour over the fish.

Black Pasta with Squid and Tomato Sauce

Tagliatelle flavoured with squid ink looks amazing and tastes deliciously of the sea. You'll find it in good Italian delicatessens and some of the larger supermarkets.

SERVES FOUR

INGREDIENTS
- 105ml/7 tbsp olive oil
- 2 shallots, chopped
- 3 garlic cloves, crushed
- 45ml/3 tbsp chopped fresh parsley
- 675g/1½lb cleaned squid, cut into rings and rinsed
- 150ml/¼ pint/⅔ cup dry white wine
- 400g/14oz can chopped tomatoes
- 2.5ml/½ tsp dried chilli flakes
- 450g/1lb squid ink tagliatelle
- salt and ground black pepper

1 Heat the oil in a pan and add the shallots. Cook until pale golden, then add the garlic. When the garlic colours a little, add 30ml/2 tbsp of the parsley, stir, then add the squid and stir again. Cook for 3–4 minutes, then pour in the wine and mix well.

2 Simmer for a few seconds, then add the tomatoes and chilli flakes, and season with salt and pepper. Cover and simmer gently for about 1 hour, until the squid is tender.

3 Fill a pan with water, add salt and bring to the boil. Cook the pasta according to the packet instructions, until *al dente*. A little oil can be added to the water to stop the pasta from sticking.

4 Remove the tagliatelle from the heat and, using a colander, drain it well, then return it to the pan. Add the squid sauce and toss over the heat with two spatulas or wooden spoons until all the strands are coated in sauce.

5 Serve in heated bowls, sprinkling each serving with a little of the remaining chopped parsley.

COOK'S TIP
The cooking time for the pasta will depend on what type you use. Dried tagliatelle generally takes 10–12 minutes; fresh pasta cooks in 2–3 minutes.

Grilled King Prawns with Romesco Sauce

This sauce, from the Catalan region of Spain, is served with fish and shellfish. Its main ingredients are tomatoes, canned pimiento, garlic and almonds.

SERVES FOUR

INGREDIENTS

24 raw king prawns (jumbo shrimp)
30–45ml/2–3 tbsp extra virgin olive oil
fresh flat leaf parsley sprigs, to garnish
lemon wedges, to serve

For the sauce
8 ripe tomatoes, preferably plum tomatoes
60ml/4 tbsp olive oil
1 onion, chopped
4 garlic cloves, chopped
1 canned pimiento, drained and chopped
2.5ml/½ tsp dried chilli flakes or chilli powder
75ml/5 tbsp fish stock or half white wine and half fish stock
30ml/2 tbsp white wine
10 blanched almonds
15ml/1 tbsp red wine vinegar
salt and ground black pepper

COOK'S TIP
A grilled red (bell) pepper, skinned and seeded, can be substituted for the canned pimiento, but don't be tempted to use a raw red pepper; it will not have the essential, smoky flavour.

1 Prepare the tomatoes. Cut a cross in the base of each tomato with a sharp knife. Place them in a heatproof bowl and cover with boiling water. After 30 seconds, lift them out with a slotted spoon and plunge them into a bowl of cold water. Drain.

2 The tomato skins will have begun to peel back. Using a very sharp knife, remove the skins, then cut each tomato in half and scoop out the seeds.

3 With a knife, chop the skinned tomato halves into pieces.

4 To make the sauce, heat 30ml/ 2 tbsp of the oil in a large pan, add the onion and three of the garlic cloves and cook until soft. Stir in the pimiento, tomatoes, chilli flakes or powder, fish stock (or mixture) and wine. Cover the pan and simmer the sauce for 30 minutes.

5 Toast the almonds under the grill (broiler) until golden. Transfer to a blender or food processor and grind coarsely.

6 Add the remaining 30ml/2 tbsp of oil, the vinegar and the last garlic clove, and process until evenly combined. Add the tomato and pimiento sauce and process until smooth. Season with salt and ground black pepper.

7 Remove the heads from the prawns, leaving them otherwise unshelled. Using a sharp knife, slit each one down the back and remove the dark vein. Rinse under cold running water, drain and pat dry on kitchen paper.

8 Preheat the grill. Toss the prawns in olive oil and place them in the grill pan. Grill (broil) for about 2 minutes on each side, until they are pink.

9 Arrange on a serving platter and garnish with the parsley sprigs. Add the lemon wedges, and offer the sauce separately in a small bowl or sauceboat. Serve immediately.

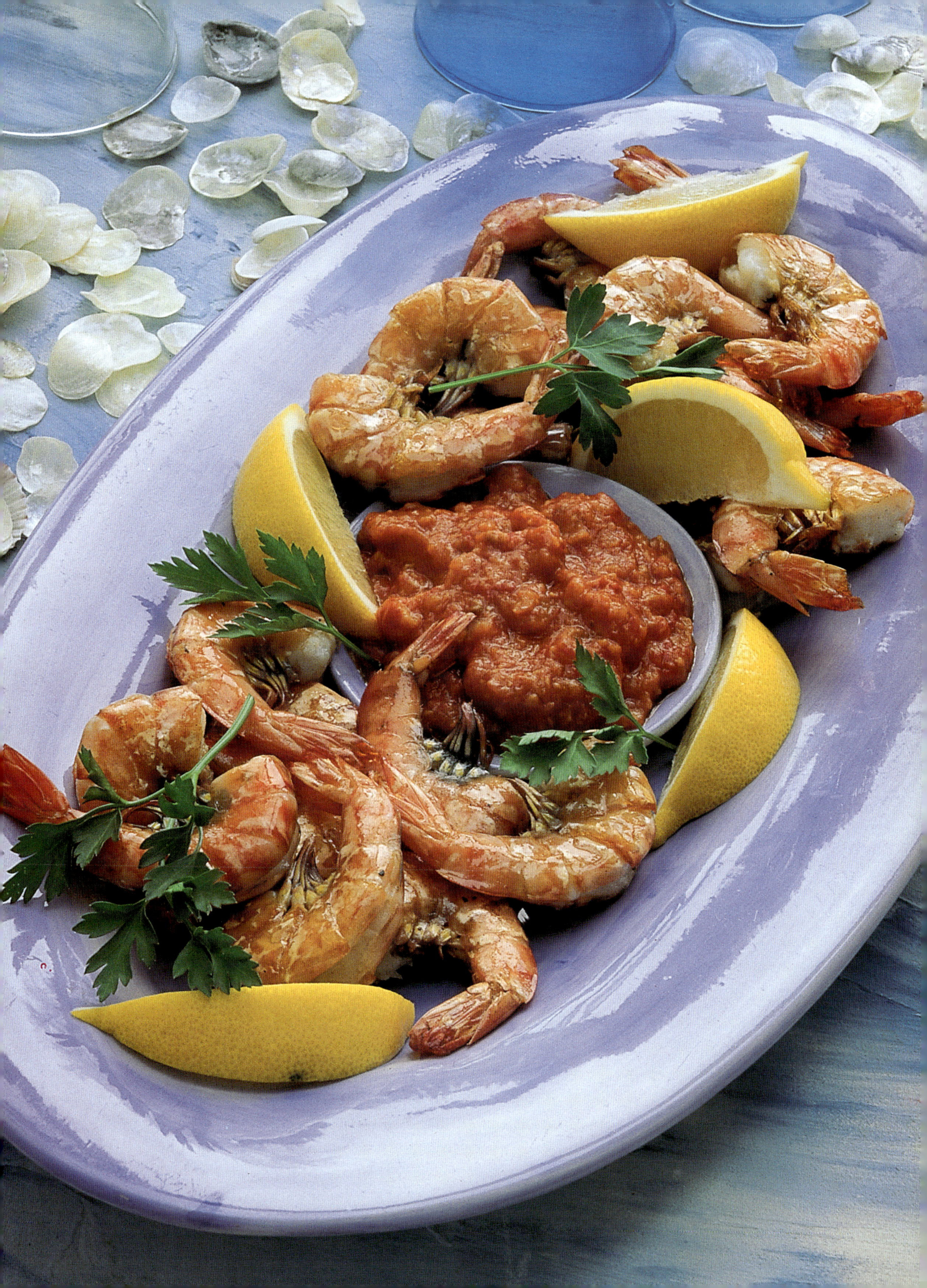

An essential ingredient in so many vegetarian dishes, tomatoes are often used as the basis for sauces — try Couscous with Eggs and Tomato Sauce or Pasta with Tomato and Chilli Sauce. They play an important role in one-pot dishes, such as warming Harvest Vegetable and Lentil Casserole or Tomato and Rich Mediterranean Vegetable Hot-pot, but it is in treats like Spicy Tomato Tart with Tomato Roses or Classic Marinara Pizza that they really take centre stage.

Vegetarian Main Meals

Baked Cheese Polenta with Tomato Sauce

POLENTA, OR CORNMEAL, IS A STAPLE FOOD IN ITALY. IT IS PREPARED LIKE A SORT OF OATMEAL, AND EATEN SOFT, OR LEFT TO SET, CUT INTO SHAPES THEN COOKED.

SERVES FOUR

INGREDIENTS
- 5ml/1 tsp salt
- 250g/9oz/1½ cups quick-cook polenta
- 5ml/1 tsp paprika
- 2.5ml/½ tsp ground nutmeg
- 30ml/2 tbsp extra virgin olive oil
- 1 large onion, finely chopped
- 2 garlic cloves, crushed
- 2 x 400g/14oz cans chopped tomatoes, or 450g/1lb fresh tomatoes
- 15ml/1 tbsp tomato purée (paste), or 30ml/2 tbsp if using fresh tomatoes
- 5ml/1 tsp granulated sugar
- salt and ground black pepper
- 75g/3oz Gruyère cheese or other mild cheese, grated

1 Preheat the oven to 200°C/400°F/Gas 6. Line a 28 x 18cm/11 x 7in baking tin (pan) with clear film. Boil 1 litre/1¾ pints/4 cups water with the salt.

2 Pour in the polenta in a steady stream and cook, stirring continuously, for 5 minutes. Beat in the paprika and nutmeg, then pour into the prepared tin and smooth the surface. Leave to cool.

3 Heat the oil in a pan and cook the onion and garlic until soft. Add the tomatoes, purée and sugar. Season. Simmer for 20 minutes.

4 Cut the polenta into 5cm/2in squares. Layer the polenta and tomato sauce in an ovenproof dish. Sprinkle with the cheese and bake for 25 minutes, until golden. Serve immediately.

LEEK, SQUASH AND TOMATO GRATIN

Colourful and succulent, you can use virtually any kind of squash for this autumn gratin, from patty pans and acorn squash to pumpkins.

SERVES FOUR TO SIX

INGREDIENTS
450g/1lb peeled and seeded squash, cut into 1cm/½in slices
60ml/4 tbsp olive oil
450g/1lb leeks, cut into thick, diagonal slices
675g/1½lb tomatoes, peeled and thickly sliced
2.5ml/½ tsp ground toasted cumin seeds
300ml/½ pint/1¼ cups single (light) cream
1 fresh red chilli, seeded and sliced
1 garlic clove, finely chopped
15ml/1 tbsp chopped fresh mint
30ml/2 tbsp chopped fresh parsley
60ml/4 tbsp fine white breadcrumbs
salt and ground black pepper

VARIATION
For a curried version of this dish, use ground coriander as well as cumin, and coconut milk instead of cream. Use fresh coriander (cilantro) instead of the mint and parsley.

1 Steam the squash over boiling salted water for 10 minutes.

2 Heat half the oil in a frying pan and cook the leeks gently for 5–6 minutes until lightly coloured. Try to keep the slices intact. Preheat the oven to 190°C/375°F/Gas 5.

3 Layer all the squash, leeks and tomatoes in a 2 litre/3½ pint/8 cup gratin dish, arranging them in rows. Season with salt, pepper and cumin.

4 Pour the cream into a small pan and add the sliced chilli and chopped garlic. Bring to the boil over a low heat then stir in the mint. Pour the mixture evenly over the layered vegetables, using a rubber spatula to scrape all the sauce out of the pan.

5 Cook for 50–55 minutes, or until the gratin is bubbling and tinged brown. Sprinkle the parsley and breadcrumbs on top and drizzle over the remaining oil. Bake for another 15–20 minutes until the breadcrumbs are browned and crisp. Serve immediately.

Tomato Bread and Butter Bake

This is a great family dish and is ideal when you don't have time to cook on the day because it can be prepared in advance. It makes a wonderful warming supper.

SERVES FOUR

INGREDIENTS

50g/2oz/¼ cup butter, softened
15ml/1 tbsp red pesto sauce
1 garlic and herb focaccia
150g/5oz mozzarella cheese, thinly sliced
2 large ripe tomatoes, sliced
300ml/½ pint/1¼ cups milk
3 large eggs
5ml/1 tsp chopped fresh oregano, plus extra to garnish
50g/2oz Pecorino Romano or Fontina cheese, grated
salt and ground black pepper

VARIATIONS
If you like, you could use other cheeses, such as Beaufort, Bel Paese or Taleggio, instead of mozzarella. A mild goat's cheese would also work well.

1 Preheat the oven to 180°C/350°F/Gas 4. Mix together the butter and pesto sauce in a small bowl. Slice the herb bread and spread one side of each slice with the pesto mixture.

2 In an oval ovenproof dish, layer the bread slices with the mozzarella and tomatoes, overlapping each new layer with the next.

3 Beat together the milk, eggs and oregano, season well and pour over the layers. Leave to stand for 5 minutes.

4 Sprinkle over the grated cheese and bake for about 40 minutes or until the top is golden brown and just set. Serve immediately, straight from the dish, sprinkled with more roughly chopped oregano.

Harvest Vegetable and Lentil Casserole

This easy-to-prepare meal is delicious served with warm garlic bread. If you really want to make the most of the tomato flavour, add a few sun-dried tomatoes with the lentils.

SERVES SIX

INGREDIENTS
- 15ml/1 tbsp sunflower oil or olive oil
- 2 leeks, sliced
- 1 garlic clove, crushed
- 4 celery sticks, chopped
- 2 carrots, sliced
- 2 parsnips, diced
- 1 sweet potato, diced
- 225g/8oz swede (rutabaga), diced
- 175g/6oz/¾ cup whole brown or green lentils
- 450g/1lb tomatoes, peeled, seeded and chopped
- 15ml/1 tbsp chopped fresh thyme
- 15ml/1 tbsp chopped fresh marjoram
- 900ml/1½ pints/3¾ cups vegetable stock
- 15ml/1 tbsp cornflour (cornstarch)
- 45ml/3 tbsp water
- salt and ground black pepper
- warm garlic bread, to serve

1 Preheat the oven to 180°C/350°F/Gas 4. Heat the sunflower oil in a large flameproof casserole. Add the prepared leeks, garlic and celery, and cook over a gentle heat for 3 minutes, stirring the vegetables occasionally.

2 Add the carrots, parsnips, sweet potato, swede, lentils, tomatoes, herbs, stock and seasoning. Stir well. Bring to the boil, stirring occasionally to ensure that the vegetables are not sticking.

3 Cover and bake for about 50 minutes until the vegetables and lentils are cooked and tender, removing the casserole from the oven and stirring the vegetable mixture once or twice during the cooking time.

4 Remove the casserole from the oven. Mix the cornflour with 45ml/3 tbsp water in a small bowl. Stir it into the casserole and heat on the hob (stovetop), stirring until the mixture comes to the boil and thickens, then simmer gently for 2 minutes, stirring. Serve in warmed bowls. Hand round garlic bread.

COOK'S TIP
Green and brown lentils, unlike red lentils, keep their shape during cooking and are good for soups, salads and casseroles. Green lentils have a delicate flavour, while brown ones are more earthy in taste.

Potato Gnocchi with Simple Tomato and Butter Sauce

Gnocchi make a substantial and tasty alternative to pasta. In this dish they are served with a very simple, but delicious, fresh tomato sauce.

SERVES FOUR

INGREDIENTS
- 675g/1½lb floury potatoes
- 2 egg yolks
- 75g/3oz/¾ cup plain (all-purpose) flour
- 60ml/4 tbsp finely chopped fresh parsley, to garnish

For the sauce
- 25g/1oz/2 tbsp butter, melted
- 450g/1lb plum tomatoes, peeled, seeded and chopped
- salt

1 Preheat the oven to 200°C/400°F/Gas 6. Scrub the potatoes, then bake them in their skins in the oven for 1 hour or until the flesh feels soft when pricked with a fork.

2 While the potatoes are still warm, cut them in half and gently squeeze the flesh into a bowl, or use a spoon to scrape the flesh out of the shells. Mash the potato well, then season with a little salt. Add the egg yolks and mix lightly with a fork or spoon.

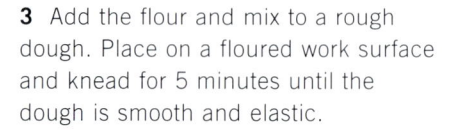

3 Add the flour and mix to a rough dough. Place on a floured work surface and knead for 5 minutes until the dough is smooth and elastic.

4 Shape the dough into small thumb-sized shapes by making long rolls and cutting them into segments. Press each of these with the back of a fork to give a ridged effect. Place the gnocchi on a floured work surface.

5 Preheat the oven to 140°C/275°F/Gas 1. Cook the gnocchi in small batches in barely simmering, slightly salted water for about 10 minutes. Remove with a slotted spoon, drain well and tip into a dish. Cover and keep hot in the oven.

6 To make the sauce, heat the butter in a small pan for 1 minute, then add the tomatoes and cook over a low heat until the juice starts to run. Sprinkle the gnocchi with chopped parsley and serve with the sauce.

Tomato and Rich Mediterranean Vegetable Hot-pot

Here's a one-dish meal that's suitable for feeding large numbers of people. It's lightly spiced and has plenty of garlic — who could refuse?

SERVES FOUR

INGREDIENTS

- 60ml/4 tbsp extra virgin olive oil or sunflower oil
- 1 large onion, chopped
- 2 small–medium aubergines (eggplant), cut into small cubes
- 4 courgettes (zucchini), cut into small chunks
- 2 red, yellow or green (bell) peppers, seeded and chopped
- 115g/4oz/1 cup fresh or frozen peas
- 115g/4oz green beans
- 200g/7oz can flageolet (small cannellini) beans, rinsed and drained
- 450g/1lb new or salad potatoes, peeled and cubed
- 2.5ml/½ tsp cinnamon
- 2.5ml/½ tsp ground cumin
- 5ml/1 tsp paprika
- 4–5 tomatoes, peeled
- 400g/14oz can chopped tomatoes
- 30ml/2 tbsp chopped fresh parsley
- 3–4 garlic cloves, crushed
- 350ml/12fl oz/1½ cups vegetable stock
- salt and ground black pepper
- black olives, to garnish
- fresh parsley, to garnish

1 Preheat the oven to 190°C/375°F/Gas 5. Heat 45ml/3 tbsp of the oil in a heavy pan, and fry the onion until golden. Add the aubergines, sauté for 3 minutes, then add the courgettes, peppers, peas, beans and potatoes, and stir in the spices and seasoning. Cook for 3 minutes, stirring constantly.

2 Cut the tomatoes in half and scoop out the seeds. Chop the tomatoes finely and place them in a bowl. Stir in the canned tomatoes with the chopped fresh parsley, crushed garlic and the remaining olive oil. Spoon the aubergine mixture into a shallow ovenproof dish and level the surface.

3 Pour the stock over the aubergine mixture and then spoon over the prepared tomato mixture.

4 Cover the dish with foil and bake for 30–45 minutes until the vegetables are tender. Serve hot, garnished with black olives and parsley.

Potato Rösti and Tofu with Fresh Tomato and Ginger Sauce

Although this dish features various components, it is not difficult to make, and the finished result is well worth the effort. Make sure you marinate the tofu for at least an hour to allow it to absorb the flavours of the ginger, garlic and tamari.

SERVES FOUR

INGREDIENTS
- 425g/15oz tofu, cut into 1cm/½in cubes
- 900g/2lb potatoes, peeled
- sunflower oil, for frying
- 30ml/2 tbsp sesame seeds, toasted
- salt and ground black pepper
- mixed leaf salad, to serve

For the marinade
- 30ml/2 tbsp tamari or dark soy sauce
- 15ml/1 tbsp clear honey
- 2 garlic cloves, crushed
- 4cm/1½in piece fresh root ginger, grated
- 5ml/1 tsp toasted sesame oil

For the sauce
- 15ml/1 tbsp olive oil
- 8 tomatoes, halved, seeded and chopped

1 Mix together all the marinade ingredients in a shallow dish and add the tofu. Spoon the marinade over the tofu and leave to marinate in the refrigerator for at least 1 hour. Turn the tofu occasionally in the marinade to allow the flavours to be absorbed.

2 To make the rösti, bring a pan of lightly salted water to the boil and par-boil the potatoes for 10–15 minutes until almost tender. Drain the potatoes well, leave to cool, then grate coarsely. Season well. Preheat the oven to 200°C/400°F/Gas 6.

3 Using a slotted spoon, remove the tofu from the marinade carefully to ensure that it does not break up. Reserve the marinade for later use. Spread out the tofu in an ovenproof dish and bake for 20 minutes, turning occasionally, until it is firm, golden and crisp on all sides.

4 Meanwhile, shape the rösti. Rinse your hands in cold water and shake them so that they are just damp. Take one-quarter of the potato mixture in your hands and form it into a rough, round cake. Repeat with the remaining mixture and shape into pieces the same size and shape as the first.

5 Heat a frying pan with just enough oil to cover the base. Place the rösti cakes in the frying pan and flatten the mixture slightly, using a wooden spatula to form rounds approximately 1cm/½in thick, though if you prefer, they can be up to 2cm/1in thick.

6 Cook the rösti over a medium heat for about 6 minutes until golden and crisp underneath. Using a fish slice or spatula, carefully turn the rösti over and cook for a further 6 minutes on the other side until they are golden brown all over.

7 Meanwhile, make the sauce. Heat the oil in a pan, add the reserved marinade and the tomatoes, and cook for 2 minutes, stirring.

8 Reduce the heat and simmer, covered, for 10 minutes, stirring occasionally, until the tomatoes break down. Press through a sieve to make a thick, smooth sauce.

9 Place a rösti on each of 4 warmed serving plates, arrange the tofu on top, spoon over the tomato sauce and sprinkle with sesame seeds. Serve with a mixed leaf salad.

COOK'S TIP
Tamari is a thick, mellow-flavoured Japanese soy sauce, which, unlike conventional Chinese soy sauce, is wheat-free and so is suitable for people who are on wheat- or gluten-free diets. It is sold in Japanese food stores and some larger health food stores.

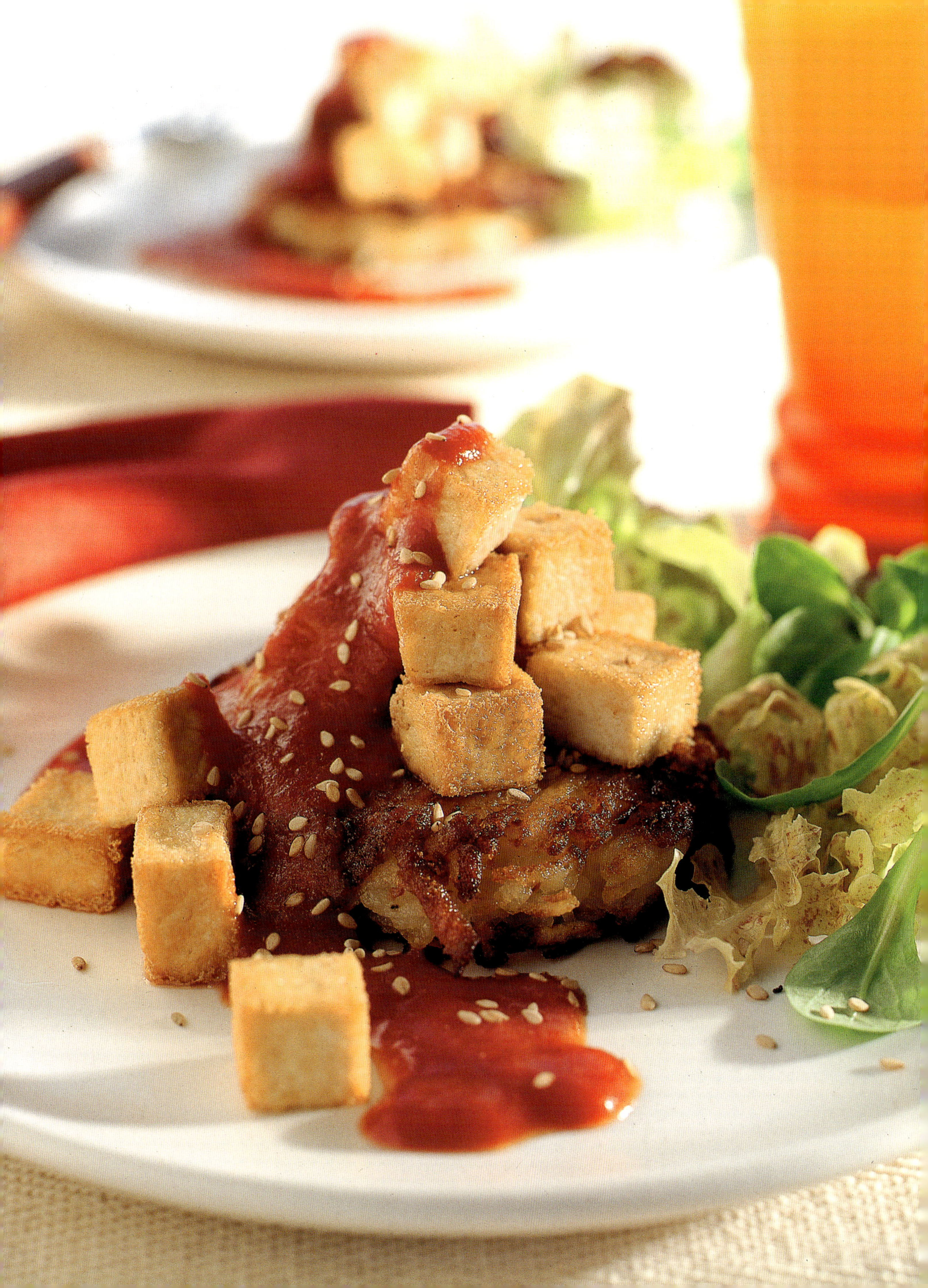

Cheese Sausages with Tomato Sauce

These are based on the Welsh speciality which are traditionally made using breadcrumbs. However, adding mashed potato lightens the sausages and makes them easier to handle.

SERVES FOUR

INGREDIENTS
- 25g/1oz/2 tbsp butter or low-fat spread
- 175g/6oz leeks or shallots, finely chopped
- 90ml/6 tbsp cold mashed potato
- 115g/4oz/2 cups fresh white or wholemeal (whole-wheat) breadcrumbs
- 150g/5oz/1¼ cups grated Caerphilly, Lancashire or Cantal cheese
- 30ml/2 tbsp chopped fresh parsley
- 5ml/1 tsp chopped fresh sage or marjoram
- 2 large eggs, beaten
- pinch of cayenne pepper
- 65g/2½oz/⅔ cup dry white breadcrumbs
- oil, for shallow frying
- salt and ground black pepper

For the sauce
- 30ml/2 tbsp extra virgin olive oil or sunflower oil
- 2 garlic cloves, thinly sliced
- 1 fresh red chilli, seeded and finely chopped, or a good pinch of dried red chilli flakes
- 1 small onion, finely chopped
- 500g/1¼lb tomatoes, peeled, seeded and chopped
- a few fresh thyme sprigs
- 10ml/2 tsp balsamic vinegar or red wine vinegar
- pinch of light muscovado (molasses) sugar
- 15–30ml/1–2 tbsp chopped fresh marjoram or oregano

VARIATION
These sausages are also delicious served with garlic mayonnaise or a confit of slow-cooked red onions.

1 Melt the butter and fry the leeks for 4–5 minutes, until softened but not browned. Tip into a bowl and add the mashed potato, fresh breadcrumbs, cheese, chopped fresh parsley and sage or marjoram. Mix well. Add sufficient beaten egg (about two-thirds of the quantity) to bind the mixture. Season well and add a good pinch of cayenne.

2 Shape the mixture into 12 sausage shapes. Dip in the remaining egg, then coat in the dry breadcrumbs. Chill the coated sausages.

3 For the sauce, heat the oil over a low heat and cook the garlic, chilli and onion for 3–4 minutes. Add the tomatoes, thyme and vinegar. Season with salt, pepper and sugar.

4 Cook the sauce for 40–50 minutes, until reduced. Remove the thyme and purée the sauce in a blender. Reheat with the marjoram or oregano, then adjust the seasoning, adding more sugar, if necessary.

5 Fry the sausages in shallow oil until golden brown on all sides. Drain on kitchen paper and serve with the sauce.

Baked Herb Crêpes with Tomato Sauce

Turn light herb crêpes into something special. Fill with a spinach, cheese and pine nut filling, then bake and serve with a delicious tomato sauce.

SERVES FOUR

INGREDIENTS
  25g/1oz/½ cup chopped fresh herbs
  15ml/1 tbsp sunflower oil, plus extra
    for frying and greasing
  120ml/4fl oz/½ cup milk
  3 eggs
  25g/1oz/¼ cup plain
    (all-purpose) flour
  pinch of salt
For the sauce
  30ml/2 tbsp olive oil
  1 small onion, chopped
  2 garlic cloves, crushed
  400g/14oz can chopped tomatoes
  pinch of soft light brown sugar
For the filling
  450g/1lb fresh spinach, cooked
    and drained
  175g/6oz/¾ cup ricotta cheese
  25g/1oz/¼ cup pine nuts, toasted
  5 sun-dried tomato halves in olive
    oil, drained and chopped
  30ml/2 tbsp shredded fresh basil
  salt, grated nutmeg and ground
    black pepper
  4 egg whites

1 To make the crêpes, place the herbs and oil in a food processor and process until smooth. Add the milk, eggs, flour and salt, and process again until smooth. Leave to rest for 30 minutes.

2 Heat a small non-stick frying pan and add a very small amount of oil. Pour out any excess oil and pour in a ladleful of the batter. Swirl around until the batter covers the base evenly.

3 Cook the crêpe for 2 minutes, turn over and cook for a further 1–2 minutes. Make 7 more crêpes in the same way.

4 To make the sauce, heat the oil in a small pan, add the onion and garlic, and cook gently for 5 minutes. Stir in the tomatoes and sugar, and cook for about 10 minutes until thickened. Purée in a blender, then sieve and set aside.

5 To make the filling, put the spinach in a bowl and add the ricotta, pine nuts, tomatoes and basil. Season with salt, nutmeg and pepper, and mix well.

6 Preheat the oven to 190°C/375°F/Gas 5. Whisk the 4 egg whites until they are stiff and stand in peaks. Stir one-third into the spinach mixture, then gently fold in the rest.

7 Place 1 crêpe at a time on a lightly oiled baking sheet, add a spoonful of filling and fold into quarters. Bake for 12 minutes until set.

8 Meanwhile, pour the tomato sauce into a small pan and reheat it gently, stirring occasionally. Serve with the crêpes.

Mexican Tortilla Parcels

Seeded green chillies add just a flicker of fire to the spicy tomato filling in these parcels, which are perfect as a main course, appetizer or snack.

SERVES FOUR

INGREDIENTS
- 675g/1½lb tomatoes
- 60ml/4 tbsp sunflower oil
- 1 large onion, finely sliced
- 1 garlic clove, crushed
- 10ml/2 tsp cumin seeds
- 2 fresh green chillies, seeded and chopped
- 30ml/2 tbsp tomato purée (paste)
- 1 vegetable stock (bouillon) cube
- 200g/7oz can corn kernels, drained
- 15ml/1 tbsp chopped fresh coriander (cilantro)
- 115g/4oz/1 cup grated Cheddar cheese
- 8 wheat tortillas
- fresh coriander (cilantro), shredded lettuce and sour cream, to serve

1 Peel the tomatoes: place them in a heatproof bowl, add boiling water to cover and leave for 30 seconds. Lift out with a slotted spoon and plunge into a bowl of cold water. Leave for 1 minute, then drain. Slip the skins off the tomatoes and chop the flesh.

2 Heat half the oil in a frying pan and fry the onion with the garlic and cumin seeds for 5 minutes, until the onion softens. Add the chillies and tomatoes, then stir in the tomato purée. Crumble the stock cube over, stir well and cook gently for 5 minutes, until the chilli is soft but the tomato has not completely broken down. Stir in the corn kernels and fresh coriander and heat gently to warm through. Keep warm.

3 Sprinkle grated cheese in the middle of each tortilla. Spoon some tomato mixture over the cheese. Fold over one edge of the tortilla, then the sides and finally the remaining edge, to enclose the filling completely.

4 Heat the remaining oil in a frying pan and fry the filled tortillas for 1–2 minutes on each side until golden and crisp. Lift them out carefully with tongs and drain on kitchen paper. Serve immediately, with coriander, shredded lettuce and sour cream.

COOK'S TIP
Mexican wheat tortillas (sometimes described as wheatflour tortillas) are available in most supermarkets. They are handy to keep in the pantry as a wrapping for a variety of vegetable mixtures.

Stuffed Beefsteak Tomatoes and Red and Yellow Peppers

Colourful peppers and tomatoes make perfect containers for various stuffings. This rice and herb version uses typically Greek ingredients.

SERVES FOUR

INGREDIENTS

2 large ripe tomatoes
1 green (bell) pepper
1 yellow or orange (bell) pepper
60ml/4 tbsp olive oil
2 onions, chopped
2 garlic cloves, crushed
115g/4oz/1 cup blanched almonds, chopped
75g/3oz/generous ½ cup long grain white rice, boiled and drained
15g/½oz fresh mint, roughly chopped
15g/½oz fresh parsley, roughly chopped
25g/1oz/3 tbsp sultanas (golden raisins)
45ml/3 tbsp ground almonds
salt and ground black pepper
chopped fresh herbs, to garnish

VARIATION
Small aubergines (eggplant) or large courgettes (zucchini) are also good for stuffing. Halve and scoop out the centres, then oil the vegetable cases and bake for about 15 minutes. Chop the centres, fry for 2–3 minutes to soften, and add to the stuffing. Fill and bake as in the main recipe.

1 Preheat the oven to 190°C/375°F/Gas 5. Cut the tomatoes in half and scoop out the pulp and seeds using a teaspoon or round-ended knife. Leave the tomato shells to drain on kitchen paper, with cut sides down. Roughly chop the tomato pulp and set it aside in a small bowl.

2 Halve the peppers, leaving the cores intact. Scoop out the seeds. Brush the peppers with 15ml/1 tbsp of the oil and bake on a baking sheet for 15 minutes. Stand the peppers and tomatoes, hollows uppermost, in a shallow ovenproof dish and season with salt and pepper.

3 Fry the onions in the remaining oil for 5 minutes. Add the garlic and chopped almonds and fry for a further 1 minute.

4 Remove the pan from the heat and stir in the rice, chopped tomato pulp, mint, parsley and sultanas. Spoon the mixture into the tomatoes and peppers.

5 Pour 150ml/¼ pint/⅔ cup boiling water around the tomatoes and peppers, and bake, uncovered, for 20 minutes. Sprinkle with the ground almonds and drizzle over a little extra olive oil. Return to the oven for a further 20 minutes. Garnish with fresh herbs.

Tomato and Lentil Dhal with Almonds

Richly flavoured with spices, coconut milk and tomatoes, this lentil dish makes a filling supper. Split red lentils give the dish a vibrant colour, but you could use larger yellow split peas instead, if you prefer.

SERVES FOUR

INGREDIENTS
- 30ml/2 tbsp vegetable oil
- 1 large onion, finely chopped
- 3 garlic cloves, chopped
- 1 carrot, diced
- 2.5cm/1in fresh root ginger, grated
- 10ml/2 tsp cumin seeds
- 10ml/2 tsp yellow mustard seeds
- 10ml/2 tsp ground turmeric
- 5ml/1 tsp mild chilli powder
- 5ml/1 tsp garam masala
- 225g/8oz/1 cup split red lentils
- 400ml/14fl oz/1⅔ cups water
- 400ml/14fl oz/1⅔ cups coconut milk
- 12 tomatoes, peeled, seeded and chopped
- juice of 2 limes
- 60ml/4 tbsp chopped fresh coriander (cilantro)
- 25g/1oz/¼ cup flaked (sliced) almonds, toasted
- salt and ground black pepper
- warmed naan bread and natural (plain) yogurt, to serve

1 Heat the oil in a large heavy pan. Sauté the chopped onion for 5 minutes until softened, stirring occasionally. Add the garlic, carrot, ginger, cumin and mustard seeds. Cook for 5 minutes, stirring, until the seeds begin to pop and the carrot softens slightly.

2 Stir in the ground turmeric, chilli powder and the garam masala, and cook for 1 minute or until the flavours mingle, stirring constantly to prevent the spices sticking and burning on the base of the pan.

3 Add the split red lentils, water, coconut milk and chopped tomatoes to the pan. Season well with salt and ground black pepper.

4 Bring to the boil, then reduce the heat and gently simmer, covered with a lid, for about 45 minutes, stirring occasionally to prevent the lentils from sticking to the base of the pan.

5 Stir in the lime juice and 45ml/3 tbsp of the fresh coriander, then check the seasoning, adding more if necessary. Cook the mixture for a further 15 minutes until the lentils soften and become tender.

6 To garnish, sprinkle with the remaining coriander and the flaked almonds. Serve with warmed naan bread and natural yogurt.

COOK'S TIPS
- It is a good idea to cover the pan while the cumin seeds and mustard seeds are popping. It is surprising how far they can travel.
- Garam masala, which means "warming spices", is a mixture of cumin seeds, cinnamon, black peppercorns and cloves. It is available ready-mixed from ethnic food stores and larger supermarkets.

Bean Feast with Tomato and Avocado Salsa

This is a very quick and easy recipe using canned beans, although it could be made with dried beans. They would need to be soaked overnight, boiled hard for 10 minutes, then simmered for 1–1½ hours until tender.

SERVES FOUR

INGREDIENTS
- 15ml/1 tbsp olive oil
- 1 small onion, finely chopped
- 3 garlic cloves, finely chopped
- 1 fresh red Ancho chilli, seeded and finely chopped
- 1 red (bell) pepper, seeded and coarsely chopped
- 2 plum tomatoes, chopped
- 2 bay leaves
- 10ml/2 tsp chopped fresh oregano
- 10ml/2 tsp ground cumin
- 5ml/1 tsp ground coriander
- 2.5ml/½ tsp ground cloves
- 15ml/1 tbsp soft dark brown sugar
- 400g/14oz can red kidney beans, rinsed and drained
- 400g/14oz can flageolet (small cannellini) beans, rinsed and drained
- 400g/14oz can borlotti beans, rinsed and drained
- 300ml/½ pint/1¼ cups vegetable stock
- salt and ground black pepper
- fresh coriander (cilantro), to garnish

For the salsa
- 1 ripe, but firm, avocado
- 45ml/3 tbsp fresh lime juice
- 1 small red onion
- 1 small fresh hot green chilli
- 5 ripe plum tomatoes
- 45ml/3 tbsp chopped fresh coriander (cilantro)

1 Heat the oil and fry the onion for 3 minutes, until transparent. Add the garlic, chilli, pepper, herbs and spices.

2 Stir well and cook for a further 3 minutes, then add the sugar, beans and stock, and cook for 8 minutes. Season with salt and plenty of ground black pepper.

3 To make the salsa, peel the avocado, cut it in half around the stone (pit), then remove the stone by striking it with the blade of a large, sharp knife and lifting it out cleanly. Cut the flesh into 1cm/½in dice. Place in a mixing bowl with the lime juice and stir to mix.

4 Chop the red onion and slice the chilli, discarding the seeds. Plunge the tomatoes into boiling water, leave for 30 seconds and then peel away the skin. Chop the tomatoes.

5 Add the onion, chilli, tomatoes and coriander to the avocado. Season with black pepper and stir to mix. Spoon the beans into a warmed serving dish or into 4 serving bowls. Serve with the tomato and avocado salsa and garnish with sprigs of fresh coriander.

Couscous with Eggs and Tomato Sauce

Middle Eastern vegetarian food is both varied and quick, especially with the easy-to-use, ready-prepared couscous that is available today.

SERVES FOUR

INGREDIENTS

- 675g/1½lb plum tomatoes, roughly chopped
- 4 garlic cloves, chopped
- 75ml/5 tbsp olive oil
- ½ fresh red chilli, seeded and chopped
- 10ml/2 tsp soft light brown sugar
- 4 eggs
- 1 large onion, chopped
- 2 celery sticks, finely sliced
- 50g/2oz/⅓ cup sultanas (golden raisins)
- 200g/7oz/generous 1 cup ready-to-use couscous
- 350ml/12fl oz/1½ cups hot vegetable stock
- salt and ground black pepper

1 Preheat the oven to 200°C/400°F/Gas 6. Spread out the tomatoes and garlic in a roasting tin (pan), drizzle with 30ml/2 tbsp of the oil, sprinkle with chopped chilli, sugar and salt and pepper, and roast for 20 minutes.

2 Cook the eggs in boiling water for 4 minutes, then plunge them straight into cold water and leave until cold. Carefully peel off the shells.

3 Heat 15–30ml/1–2 tbsp of the remaining olive oil in a large pan and fry the onion and celery until softened. Add the sultanas, couscous and hot stock, and set aside until all the liquid has been absorbed. Stir gently, adding extra hot stock if necessary, and season to taste. Tip the mixture into a large heated serving dish, bury the eggs in the couscous and cover with foil. Keep warm in the oven.

4 Remove the tomato mixture from the oven and press it through a sieve placed over a bowl. Add 15ml/1 tbsp boiling water and the rest of the olive oil and stir to make a smooth, rich sauce.

5 Remove the couscous mixture from the oven and locate the eggs. Spoon a little tomato sauce over the top of each egg. Serve immediately, with the rest of the sauce handed separately.

Hot Vegetable Couscous with Harissa

A North African favourite, this deliciously spicy dish, made rich with tomatoes and prunes, makes an excellent and unusual meal for vegetarians.

SERVES FOUR

INGREDIENTS

    45ml/3 tbsp extra virgin olive oil or sunflower oil
    1 onion, chopped
    2 garlic cloves, crushed
    5ml/1 tsp ground cumin
    5ml/1 tsp paprika
    400g/14oz can chopped tomatoes
    300ml/½ pint/1¼ cups vegetable stock
    1 cinnamon stick
    generous pinch of saffron threads
    4 baby aubergines (eggplant), quartered
    8 baby courgettes (zucchini), trimmed
    8 baby carrots
    225g/8oz/1⅓ cups couscous, soaked
    400g/14oz can chickpeas, rinsed and drained
    175g/6oz/¾ cup prunes
    45ml/3 tbsp chopped fresh parsley
    45ml/3 tbsp chopped fresh coriander (cilantro)
    10–15ml/2–3 tsp harissa
    salt

COOK'S TIPS
• Harissa is a very hot chilli sauce from North Africa. It looks rather like puréed tomatoes but needs to be treated with a great deal more caution. Use it sparingly.
• When choosing a steamer, metal sieve or colander for steaming the couscous, check that it fits neatly over the pan in which you intend to cook the vegetables.

1 Heat the olive oil in a large pan. Add the onion and garlic, and cook gently for 5 minutes until soft. Add the cumin and paprika and cook, stirring, for 1 minute.

2 Add the tomatoes, stock, cinnamon stick, saffron, aubergines, courgettes and carrots, with water to cover. Season with salt. Bring to the boil, cover, lower the heat and cook for 20 minutes until the vegetables are just tender.

3 Line a medium size steamer with muslin (cheesecloth). Steam the couscous according to the instructions on the packet. Add the chickpeas and prunes to the vegetables and cook for 5 minutes.

4 Place the couscous on top of the vegetable pan, cover, and cook for 5 minutes until the couscous is hot.

5 Stir the parsley and coriander into the vegetables. Heap the couscous on to a serving plate. Using a slotted spoon, arrange the vegetables over the couscous. Spoon over a little of the remaining liquid and combine.

6 Stir the harissa into the remaining reserved liquor and serve separately.

Mexican Rice

Versions of this dish — a relative of Spanish rice — are popular all over Latin America. It is a delicious medley of rice, tomatoes and aromatic flavourings.

SERVES SIX

INGREDIENTS

200g/7oz/1 cup long grain rice
400g/14oz can chopped tomatoes in tomato juice
½ onion, roughly chopped
2 garlic cloves, roughly chopped
30ml/2 tbsp vegetable oil, preferably olive oil
225ml/⅖ pint/scant 1 cup vegetable stock
2.5ml/½ tsp salt
3 fresh chillies
150g/5oz/1 cup frozen peas
ground black pepper

1 Put the rice in a large heatproof bowl and pour over boiling water to cover. Stir once, then leave to stand for 10 minutes. Tip into a strainer over the sink, rinse under cold water, then drain again. Set aside to dry slightly.

2 Meanwhile, pour the tomatoes and juice into a food processor or blender, add the onion and garlic, and process until smooth.

3 Heat the oil in a large, heavy pan, add the rice and cook over a medium heat until the rice becomes a delicate golden brown colour. Stir occasionally with a wooden spatula to ensure that the rice does not stick to the base of the pan.

4 Add the tomato mixture and stir over a medium heat until all the liquid has been absorbed. Stir in the stock, salt, whole chillies and peas. Continue to cook the mixture, stirring occasionally, until all the liquid has been absorbed and the rice is just tender.

5 Remove the pan from the heat, cover it with a tight-fitting lid and leave it to stand in a warm place for 5–10 minutes. Remove the chillies, fluff up the rice lightly with a fork, and serve in warmed bowls, sprinkled with black pepper. The chillies may be used as a garnish, if you like.

COOK'S TIP
Do not stir the rice too often after adding the stock or the grains will break down and the mixture will become starchy.

Tomato Rice

Proof positive that you don't need elaborate ingredients or complicated cooking methods to make a delicious dish.

SERVES FOUR

INGREDIENTS
- 30ml/2 tbsp sunflower oil
- 2.5ml/½ tsp onion seeds
- 1 onion, sliced
- 4 tomatoes, sliced
- 1 orange or yellow (bell) pepper, seeded and sliced
- 5ml/1 tsp grated fresh root ginger
- 1 garlic clove
- 5ml/1 tsp chilli powder
- 1 potato, diced
- 7.5ml/1½ tsp salt
- 400g/14oz/2 cups basmati rice, soaked
- 750ml/1¼ pints/3 cups water
- 30–45ml/2–3 tbsp chopped fresh coriander (cilantro)

1 Heat the oil and fry the onion seeds for about 30 seconds. Add the sliced onion and fry for about 5 minutes.

2 Stir in the tomatoes, pepper, ginger, garlic, chilli powder, diced potato and salt. Stir-fry over a medium heat for about 5 minutes more.

3 Drain the rice and add it to the pan, then stir for about 1 minute until the grains are well coated. Pour in the water and bring the rice to the boil, then lower the heat, give the mixture a stir, cover the pan and cook the rice for 12–15 minutes.

4 Remove the pan from the heat, without lifting the lid, and leave the rice to stand for 5 minutes. Stir in the chopped coriander. Serve in warmed bowls, forking the rice over gently as you do so. If you like, sprinkle a little extra coriander on top of each portion.

Tomato Rice and Beans with Avocado Salsa

Mexican-style rice and beans make a delicious supper dish. Spoon on to tortillas and serve with a tangy salsa. Alternatively, serve as an accompaniment to a spicy stew.

SERVES FOUR

INGREDIENTS

- 40g/1½oz/¼ cup dried or 75g/3oz/½ cup canned kidney beans, rinsed and drained
- 8 tomatoes, halved and seeded
- 2 garlic cloves, chopped
- 1 onion, sliced
- 45ml/3 tbsp olive oil
- 225g/8oz/generous 1 cup long grain brown rice, rinsed
- 600ml/1 pint/2½ cups vegetable stock
- 2 carrots, diced
- 75g/3oz/¾ cup green beans
- salt and ground black pepper
- 4 wheat tortillas and sour cream, to serve

For the avocado salsa
- 1 avocado
- juice of 1 lime
- 1 small red onion, diced
- 1 small fresh red chilli, seeded and chopped
- 15ml/1 tbsp chopped fresh coriander (cilantro)

1 If using dried kidney beans, place in a bowl, cover with cold water and leave to soak overnight, then drain and rinse well. Place in a pan with enough water to cover and bring to the boil. Boil rapidly for 10 minutes, then reduce the heat. Simmer for 40–50 minutes until tender; drain and set aside.

2 Make the avocado salsa. Halve and stone (pit) the avocado. Peel and dice the flesh, then toss it in the lime juice. Add the onion, chilli and coriander. Mix well.

3 Preheat the grill (broiler) to high. Place the tomatoes, garlic and onion on a baking tray. Pour over 15ml/1 tbsp of the oil and toss to coat. Grill (broil) for 10 minutes or until the tomatoes and onions are softened, turning once. Set aside to cool. Heat the remaining oil in a pan, add the rice and cook for 2 minutes, stirring, until light golden.

4 Purée the cooled tomatoes and onion in a food processor or blender, then add the mixture to the rice and cook for a further 2 minutes, stirring frequently. Pour in the vegetable stock, then cover and cook gently for 20 minutes, stirring occasionally.

5 Stir 30ml/2 tbsp of the kidney beans into the salsa. Add the rest to the rice mixture with the carrots and green beans, and cook for 10 minutes until the vegetables are tender. Season well. Remove the pan from the heat and leave to stand, covered, for 15 minutes.

6 Warm the wheat tortillas and place one on each serving plate. Spoon the hot rice and bean mixture on top. Serve immediately, with the avocado salsa and a bowl of sour cream.

Pasta with Tomato and Chilli Sauce

This dish comes from Lazio, in Italy, where it is described as "all'arrabbiata" which means angry – it describes the heat that comes from the chilli.

SERVES FOUR

INGREDIENTS

   500g/1¼lb sugocasa (see Cook's Tip)
   2 garlic cloves, crushed
   150ml/¼ pint/⅔ cup dry white wine
   15ml/1 tbsp sun-dried tomato paste
   1 fresh red chilli
   300g/11oz/2¾ cups penne or tortiglioni
   60ml/4 tbsp finely chopped fresh flat leaf parsley
   salt and ground black pepper
   freshly grated Pecorino cheese, to serve

COOK'S TIP
Sugocasa resembles passata (bottled strained tomatoes), but is rougher.

1 Mix the sugocasa, garlic, wine, sun-dried tomato paste and whole chilli in a pan and bring to the boil. Cover and simmer gently, stirring.

2 Drop the pasta into a large pan of rapidly boiling salted water. Lower the heat and simmer for 10–12 minutes or until *al dente*.

3 Remove the chilli from the sauce and add 30ml/2 tbsp of the parsley. Taste for seasoning. If you prefer a hotter taste, chop some or all of the chilli and return it to the sauce.

4 Drain the pasta and tip it into a warmed large bowl. Pour the sauce over the pasta and toss to mix. Serve at once, sprinkled with grated Pecorino and the remaining parsley.

Paglia e Fieno with Sun-dried Tomatoes and Radicchio

This is a light, modern pasta dish of the kind served in fashionable restaurants. It is the presentation that sets it apart, the careful drizzling of the tomato sauce and placing of pasta, not the usual quick-and-easy preparation.

SERVES FOUR TO SIX

INGREDIENTS
- 45ml/3 tbsp extra virgin olive oil or sunflower oil
- 30ml/2 tbsp sun-dried tomato paste
- 2 pieces drained sun-dried tomatoes in olive oil, cut into very thin slivers
- 40g/1½oz radicchio leaves, finely shredded
- 45ml/3 tbsp pine nuts
- 350g/12oz *paglia e fieno* (or two different colours of tagliatelle)
- 4–6 spring onions (scallions), thinly sliced into rings
- salt and freshly ground black pepper

1 Heat 15ml/1 tbsp of the oil in a medium pan or frying pan. Add the sun-dried tomato paste and the sun-dried tomatoes, then stir in 2 ladlefuls of water.

2 Allow the sauce to simmer on a low heat until it is slightly reduced, stirring constantly to prevent sticking.

3 Mix in the shredded radicchio, then taste and season if necessary. Keep on a low heat.

4 Put the pine nuts in a non-stick frying pan and toss over a low to medium heat for 1–2 minutes or until they are lightly toasted and golden. Remove and set aside.

5 Cook the pasta according to the packet instructions, keeping the colours separate by using two pans. Drain and return the pasta to the separate pans. Add about 15ml/1 tbsp oil to each pan and toss over a medium to high heat until the pasta is glistening with the oil.

6 Arrange a portion of green and white pasta in each of 4–6 warmed bowls, then spoon the sun-dried tomato and radicchio mixture in the centre. Sprinkle the spring onions and pine nuts over the top and serve immediately. Before eating, each diner should toss the sauce ingredients with the pasta.

COOK'S TIP
If you find the presentation too fussy, you can toss the tomato and radicchio mixture with the pasta in a large bowl before serving, then sprinkle the spring onions and toasted pine nuts on top.

Vegetarian Main Meals 135

Rigatoni with Tomatoes, Wild Mushrooms and Fresh Herbs

This is a good sauce to make from store-cupboard ingredients because it doesn't rely on anything fresh, apart from the shallots and herbs. It is perfect for the end-of-week meal when you have run out of food and energy for cooking.

SERVES FOUR

INGREDIENTS

- 2 x 15g/½oz packets dried wild mushrooms
- 175ml/6fl oz/¾ cup warm water
- 30ml/2 tbsp olive oil
- 2 shallots, finely chopped
- 2 garlic cloves, crushed
- a few sprigs of fresh marjoram, chopped, plus extra to garnish
- 1 handful fresh flat leaf parsley, chopped
- 25g/1oz/2 tbsp cold butter
- 400g/14oz can chopped tomatoes
- 400g/14oz/3½ cups dried rigatoni
- 25g/1oz/⅓ cup freshly grated Parmesan cheese, plus extra to serve
- salt and ground black pepper

1 Put the dried mushrooms in a bowl, pour the warm water over to cover and soak for 15–20 minutes. Tip into a fine sieve set over a bowl and squeeze the mushrooms with your fingers to release as much liquid as possible. Reserve the mushrooms and the strained liquid.

2 Heat the oil in a medium frying pan and fry the shallots, garlic and herbs over a low heat, stirring frequently, for about 5 minutes. Add the mushrooms and butter, and stir until the butter has melted. Season well.

3 Stir in the tomatoes and the reserved liquid from the soaked mushrooms. Bring to the boil, then cover, lower the heat and simmer for about 20 minutes, stirring occasionally. Meanwhile, cook the pasta according to the instructions on the packet.

4 Taste the sauce for seasoning. Drain the pasta, reserving some of the cooking water, and tip it into a warmed large bowl. Add the sauce and the grated Parmesan and toss to mix. Add a little cooking water if you prefer a runnier sauce. Serve immediately, garnished with marjoram and with more Parmesan cheese, which can be handed around separately.

VARIATIONS
- If you have a bottle of wine open, red or white, add a splash when you add the canned tomatoes.
- For a richer sauce, add a few tablespoonfuls of cream or mascarpone to the sauce just before serving.

Vegetable Tarte Tatin

Savoury upside-down tarts are becoming increasingly popular. This one combines Mediterranean vegetables with a medley of rice, garlic, onions and olives.

SERVES TWO

INGREDIENTS
- 30ml/2 tbsp sunflower oil
- 25ml/1½ tbsp olive oil
- 1 aubergine (eggplant), sliced lengthways
- 1 large red (bell) pepper, seeded and cut into long strips
- 10 tomatoes
- 2 red shallots, finely chopped
- 1–2 garlic cloves, crushed
- 150ml/¼ pint/⅔ cup white wine
- 10ml/2 tsp chopped fresh basil
- 225g/8oz/2 cups cooked white or brown long grain rice
- 40g/1½oz/scant ½ cup pitted black olives, chopped
- 350g/12oz puff pastry, thawed if frozen
- ground black pepper
- salad leaves, to serve

COOK'S TIP
This tart would make a lovely lunch or supper dish. Serve it hot with buttered new potatoes and a green vegetable, such as mangetouts (snow peas), sugarsnap peas or green beans.

1 Preheat the oven to 190°C/375°F/Gas 5. Heat the sunflower oil with 15ml/1 tbsp of the olive oil in a frying pan and fry the aubergine slices, in batches if necessary, for 4–5 minutes on each side until golden brown. As each aubergine slice softens and browns, lift it out and drain on several sheets of kitchen paper to remove as much oil as possible.

2 Add the pepper strips to the oil remaining in the pan, turning them to coat. Cover the pan with a lid or foil and sweat the peppers over a medium high heat for 5–6 minutes, stirring occasionally, until the pepper strips are soft and flecked with brown.

3 Slice two of the tomatoes and set them aside.

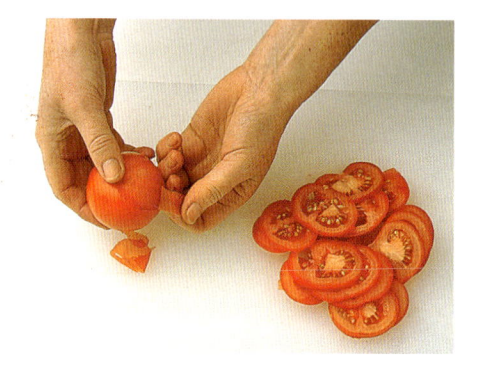

4 Plunge the remaining tomatoes into boiling water for 30 seconds, then drain. Peel them, cut them into quarters and remove the core and seeds. Chop them roughly.

5 Heat the remaining oil in the frying pan and fry the shallots and garlic for 3–4 minutes until softened. Add the chopped tomatoes and cook for a few minutes until softened.

6 Stir in the wine and basil, with black pepper to taste. Bring to the boil, then remove from the heat and stir in the cooked rice and pitted black olives, making sure they are well distributed.

7 Arrange the tomato slices, aubergine slices and peppers in a single layer over the base of a heavy, 30cm/12in shallow ovenproof dish. Spread the rice mixture on top.

8 Roll out the pastry to a circle slightly larger than the diameter of the dish and place it on top of the rice, tucking the overlap down inside the dish.

9 Bake for 25–30 minutes, until the pastry is golden and risen. Cool slightly, then invert the tart on to a large, warmed serving plate. Serve in slices, with a leafy green salad or simply dressed lamb's lettuce or mâche.

VARIATIONS
- Use large courgettes (zucchini) instead of aubergine slices.
- Instead of using only red pepper, use a mixture of red, yellow and orange.
- Red shallots can be hard to come by; substitute 1 red onion.
- Omit the black olives and add currants instead.

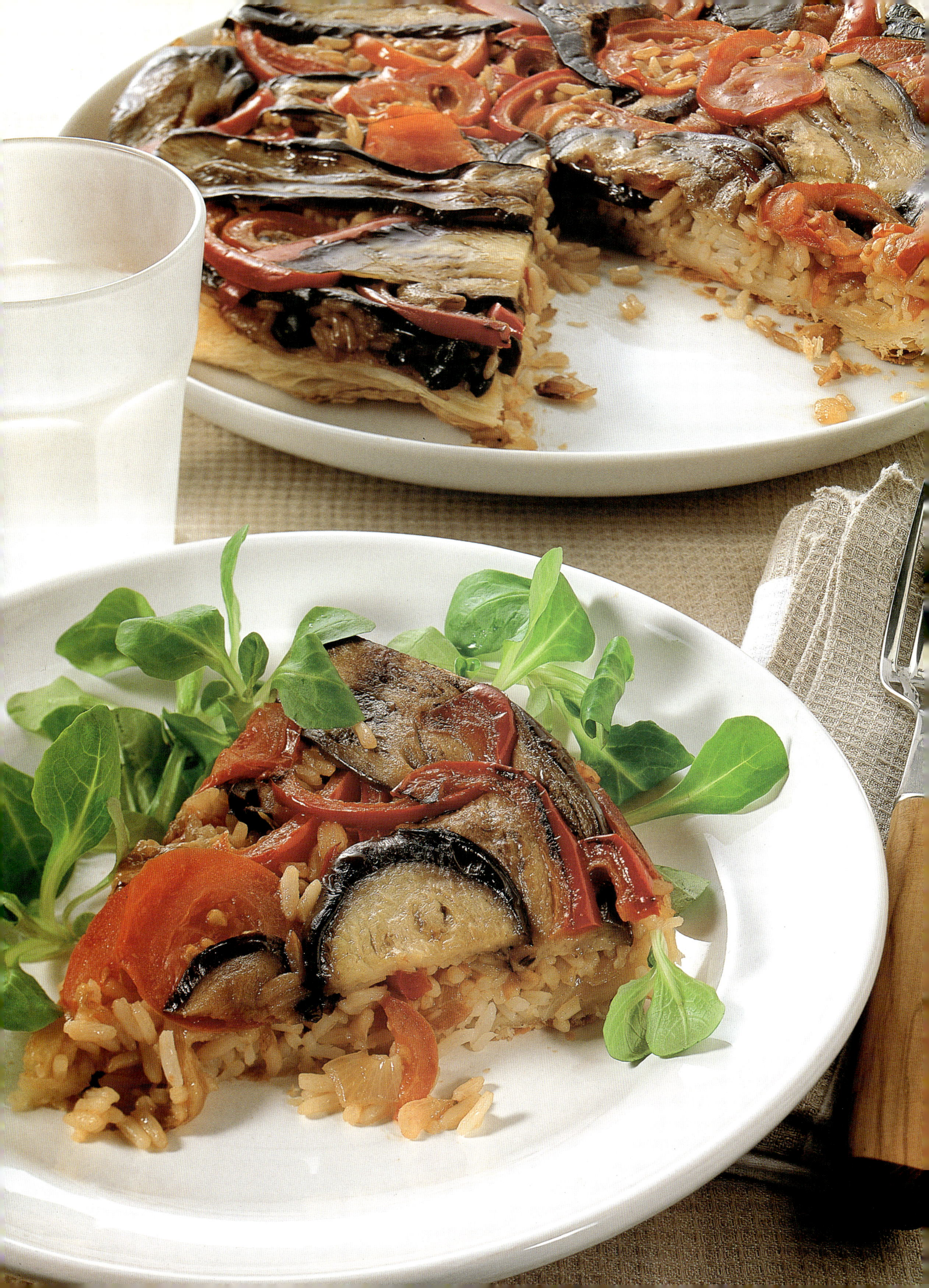

Tomato and Basil Tart

THIS IS A VERY SIMPLE YET EXTREMELY TASTY TART MADE WITH RICH SHORTCRUST PASTRY, TOPPED WITH SLICES OF MOZZARELLA CHEESE AND TOMATOES, DRIZZLED WITH OLIVE OIL AND DOTTED WITH FRESH BASIL LEAVES. IT TASTES BEST HOT.

SERVES FOUR

INGREDIENTS

150g/5oz mozzarella cheese, thinly sliced
4 large tomatoes, thickly sliced
about 10 fresh basil leaves
30ml/2 tbsp olive oil
2 garlic cloves, thinly sliced
sea salt and ground black pepper

For the pastry
115g/4oz/1 cup plain (all-purpose) flour, plus extra for dusting
pinch of salt
50g/2oz/¼ cup butter, at room temperature
1 egg yolk, cold

1 To prepare the pastry, sift the flour and salt into a bowl. Rub in the butter until the mixture resembles fine breadcrumbs. Beat the egg yolk and add to the crumb-like mixture. Add a little water at a time, and mix together until the dough is smooth. Knead lightly on a floured work surface for a few minutes. Place in a plastic bag and chill for about 1 hour in a refrigerator.

2 Preheat the oven to 190°C/375°F/Gas 5. Remove the pastry from the refrigerator, allow about 10 minutes for it to return to room temperature and then roll out into a 20cm/8in round. The pastry should be an even thickness all over.

3 Press the pastry into a 20cm/8in flan tin (tart pan). Bake in the oven for 10 minutes. Allow to cool. Reduce the oven temperature to 180°C/350°F/Gas 4.

4 Arrange the mozzarella slices over the pastry. On top, arrange the sliced tomatoes. Dip the basil leaves in olive oil and arrange them on the tomatoes.

5 Sprinkle the garlic on top, drizzle with the remaining oil and season. Bake the tart for 45 minutes, or until the pastry case is golden brown and tomatoes are well cooked. Serve hot.

Spicy Tomato Tart with Tomato Roses

Serve this chilli-flavoured tomato tart hot or cold with a fresh, crispy salad. For an impressive finishing touch, garnish with pretty tomato roses.

SERVES EIGHT TO TEN

INGREDIENTS
- 300g/11oz/2¾ cups self-raising (self-rising) flour
- 200g/7oz/scant 1 cup butter, diced
- 45–60ml/3–4 tbsp cold water
- salt and ground black pepper
- tomato roses and a sprig of basil, to garnish

For the filling
- 30ml/2 tbsp olive oil
- 2 onions, thinly sliced
- 1 garlic clove, crushed
- 1.3–1.6kg/3–3½lb tomatoes, peeled and chopped
- 2 dried chillies, seeded and chopped
- 120ml/4fl oz/½ cup passata (bottled strained tomatoes)
- 30ml/2 tbsp sugar

1 Place the flour, a pinch of salt and the butter in a food processor or blender; process into breadcrumbs.

2 Add the water and process for 5–10 seconds. Turn out on to a floured work surface and knead to a firm dough. Wrap in clear film (plastic wrap) and chill for 30 minutes. Preheat the oven to 190°C/375°F/Gas 5.

3 Make the filling. Heat the olive oil in a large frying pan, add the onions and garlic and fry for 10 minutes. Stir in the chopped tomatoes and chillies. Bring to the boil, lower the heat and simmer for 20–25 minutes until thickened. Add the passata and sugar, and simmer for 5 minutes more. Season and cool.

4 On a lightly floured work surface, roll out the pastry and line a deep 25cm/10in flan tin (tart pan). Prick the base of the pastry, line with baking parchment and fill with baking beans. Bake blind for 15 minutes, then remove the beans and paper. Return the flan tin to the oven for a further 5 minutes.

5 Pour the tomato sauce into the pastry case, spreading it out evenly. Return the tomato tart to the oven and bake for 20–25 minutes.

6 Serve the tomato tart hot or at room temperature. Garnish with tomato roses and a sprig of basil.

Mushroom, Corn and Plum Tomato Wholewheat Pizza

This tasty vegetable pizza can be served hot or cold with a mixed bean salad and fresh crusty bread or baked potatoes. It is also ideal for picnics or packed lunches.

SERVES TWO

INGREDIENTS

    30ml/2 tbsp tomato purée (paste)
    10ml/2 tsp dried basil
    10ml/2 tsp olive oil
    1 onion, sliced
    1 garlic clove, crushed or finely chopped
    2 small courgettes (zucchini), sliced
    115g/4oz mushrooms, sliced
    115g/4oz/⅔ cup canned or frozen corn kernels
    4 plum tomatoes, sliced
    50g/2oz/½ cup Red Leicester cheese, finely grated
    50g/2oz mozzarella cheese, finely grated
    salt and ground black pepper
    basil sprigs, to garnish
    mixed bean salad and fresh crusty bread or baked potatoes, to serve

For the pizza base
    225g/8oz/2 cups plain wholemeal (all-purpose whole-wheat) flour
    pinch of salt
    10ml/2 tsp baking powder
    50g/2oz/4 tbsp margarine
    about 150ml/¼ pint/⅔ cup milk

1 Preheat the oven to 220°C/425°F/Gas 7. Grease a baking sheet with a little oil. Put the flour, salt and baking powder in a bowl and rub the margarine lightly into the flour until it resembles breadcrumbs.

2 Add enough milk to form a soft dough and knead. Roll the dough out to a circle about 25cm/10in in diameter.

3 Place the dough on the prepared baking sheet and make the edges slightly thicker than the centre. Spread the tomato purée over the base and sprinkle the basil on top.

4 Heat the oil in a frying pan, add the onion, garlic, courgettes and mushrooms, and cook gently for 10 minutes, stirring occasionally.

5 Spread the hot vegetable mixture over the pizza base, sprinkle over the corn kernels and season with salt and ground black pepper. Arrange the tomato slices on top.

6 Mix together the Red Leicester and mozzarella cheeses and sprinkle over the pizza. Bake for 25–30 minutes, until the dough is cooked and the cheese is golden brown. Serve the pizza hot or cold in slices, garnished with basil sprigs, with bean salad and crusty bread or baked potatoes.

Classic Marinara Pizza

The combination of simple ingredients, fresh garlic, good-quality olive oil and a fresh tomato sauce gives this pizza an unmistakably Italian flavour. Although plain in looks, the taste of the marinara is utterly delicious.

SERVES TWO

INGREDIENTS
- 60ml/4 tbsp extra virgin olive oil or sunflower oil
- 675g/1½lb plum tomatoes, peeled, seeded and chopped
- 4 garlic cloves, cut into slivers
- 15ml/1 tbsp chopped fresh oregano
- salt and ground black pepper

For the pizza base
- 225g/8oz/2 cups plain (all-purpose) white flour
- pinch of salt
- 10ml/2 tsp baking powder
- 50g/2oz/4 tbsp margarine
- about 150ml/¼ pint/⅔ cup milk

1 Preheat the oven to 220°C/425°F/Gas 7. Use non-stick baking parchment to line a baking sheet. Sieve the flour, salt and baking powder in a bowl and rub the margarine lightly into the flour until it resembles breadcrumbs.

2 Pour in enough milk to form a soft dough and knead. Roll the dough out to a circle about 25cm/10in in diameter.

3 Place the dough on the prepared baking sheet and make the edges slightly thicker than the centre.

4 Heat 30ml/2 tbsp of the oil in a pan. Add the seeded and chopped plum tomatoes and cook, stirring frequently, for about 5 minutes until soft.

5 Place the tomatoes in a sieve over a bowl and leave to drain for about 5 minutes.

6 Empty the juice from the bowl and force the tomatoes through the sieve, into the bowl with the back of a spoon. You may also use a food processor or blender and process the tomatoes until smooth.

7 Brush the pizza base with half the remaining oil. Spoon over the tomatoes and sprinkle with garlic and oregano. Drizzle over the remaining oil and season with salt and pepper.

8 Bake for 15–20 minutes in the oven until the pizza is crisp and golden. Serve immediately.

To give savoury dishes a kick, serve some salsa — from mild Aromatic Guacamole to Fiery Salsa, there are many variations on the basic theme. As for cold meats and cheeses, they become much more interesting when served with a dollop of Green Tomato Chutney or a spoonful of Apple and Tomato Chutney. Try Thousand Island Dip or Sour Cream Dip with tortilla chips for a delicious party snack.

Salsas, Relishes and Dips

Orange, Tomato and Chive Salsa

FRESH CHIVES AND SWEET ORANGES PROVIDE A VERY CHEERFUL COMBINATION OF FLAVOURS. AN UNUSUAL SALSA THAT IS A VERY GOOD ACCOMPANIMENT TO SALADS.

SERVES FOUR

INGREDIENTS
- 2 large, sweet oranges
- 1 beefsteak tomato, or 2 plum tomatoes if not available
- bunch of fresh chives
- 1 garlic clove
- 30ml/2 tbsp extra virgin olive oil or grapeseed oil
- sea salt

1 Slice the base off 1 orange so that it will stand firmly on a chopping board. Using a large sharp knife, remove the peel by slicing from the top to the bottom of the orange. Repeat with the second orange.

2 Working over a bowl, segment each orange in turn. Slice towards the middle of the fruit, and slightly to one side of a segment, and then gently twist the knife to release the orange segment. Repeat. Squeeze any juice from the remaining membrane.

3 Roughly chop the orange segments and add them to the bowl with the collected orange juice. Halve the tomato and use a teaspoon to scoop the seeds into the bowl. With a sharp knife, finely dice the flesh and add to the oranges and juice in the bowl.

4 Hold the bunch of chives neatly together and use a pair of kitchen scissors to snip them into the bowl.

5 Thinly slice the garlic and stir it into the orange mixture. Pour over the olive oil, season with sea salt and stir well to mix. Serve the salsa within 2 hours.

Smoky Tomato Salsa

The smoky flavour in this recipe comes from the smoked bacon and the commercial liquid smoke marinade. Served with sour cream, this salsa makes a great baked potato filler.

SERVES FOUR

INGREDIENTS
- 450g/1lb tomatoes
- 4 rindless smoked streaky (fatty) bacon strips
- 15ml/1 tbsp vegetable oil
- 45ml/3 tbsp chopped fresh coriander (cilantro) leaves or parsley
- 1 garlic clove, finely chopped
- 15ml/1 tbsp liquid smoke marinade
- freshly squeezed juice of 1 lime
- salt and ground black pepper

1 Plunge the tomatoes into boiling water for 30 seconds. Remove with a slotted spoon, dunk in cold water and then remove the skins. Halve the tomatoes, scoop out and discard the seeds, then finely dice the flesh.

2 Cut the bacon into small pieces. Heat the oil in a frying pan and cook the bacon for 5 minutes, stirring occasionally, until crisp and browned. Remove from the heat and drain on kitchen paper. Leave to cool for a few minutes, then place in a mixing bowl.

3 Add the finely diced tomatoes and the chopped fresh coriander or parsley to the bowl. Stir in the finely chopped garlic, then add the liquid smoke and freshly squeezed lime juice. Season the salsa with salt and pepper to taste and mix well, using a wooden spoon or plastic spatula.

4 Spoon the smoky salsa into a serving bowl, cover with clear film and chill until ready to serve.

VARIATION
Give this smoky salsa an extra kick by adding a dash of Tabasco sauce or a pinch of dried chilli flakes.

Fiery Salsa

This is a scorchingly hot salsa for only the very brave! Spread it sparingly on to cooked meats and burgers or add a tiny amount to a curry or pot of chilli.

SERVES FOUR TO SIX

INGREDIENTS
- 6 Scotch bonnet chillies
- 2 ripe tomatoes
- 4 standard green jalapeño chillies
- 30ml/2 tbsp chopped fresh parsley
- 30ml/2 tbsp olive oil
- 15ml/1 tbsp balsamic vinegar or sherry vinegar
- salt

1 Skin the Scotch bonnet chillies, either by holding them in a gas flame for 3 minutes until the skin blackens and blisters, or by plunging them into boiling water. Then, using rubber gloves, rub off the skin from the chilli.

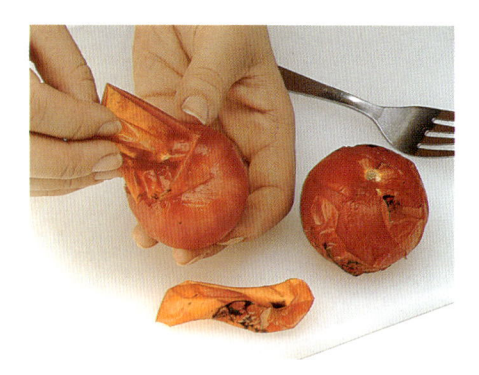

2 Hold each tomato in a gas flame for 3 minutes until the skin starts to come away (or plunge them into boiling water, if you prefer). Remove the skins, halve the tomatoes, and remove the seeds. Chop the flesh very finely.

3 Try not to touch the Scotch bonnet chillies with your bare hands: use a fork to hold them and slice them open with a sharp knife. Scrape out and discard the seeds, then finely chop the flesh.

4 Halve the jalapeño chillies, remove their seeds and finely slice them widthways into tiny strips. Mix both types of chillies, the tomatoes and the chopped parsley in a bowl.

5 In a small bowl, whisk the olive oil with the vinegar and a little salt. Pour this over the salsa and cover the dish. Chill for up to 3 days.

Bloody Mary Salsa

Serve this perfect party salsa with sticks of crunchy celery or fingers of cucumber or, on a really special occasion, with freshly shucked oysters.

SERVES TWO

INGREDIENTS
- 4 ripe tomatoes
- 1 celery stick
- 1 garlic clove
- 2 spring onions (scallions)
- 45ml/3 tbsp tomato juice
- Worcestershire sauce, to taste
- Tabasco sauce, to taste
- 10ml/2 tsp horseradish sauce
- 15ml/1 tbsp vodka
- 1 lemon
- salt and ground black pepper

VARIATION
Blend 1–2 seeded, fresh red chillies with the tomatoes, instead of stirring in the Tabasco sauce.

1 Halve the tomatoes, celery and garlic. Trim the spring onions.

2 Put the tomatoes, celery, garlic and spring onions in a blender or food processor. Process until finely chopped, then transfer the vegetable mixture to a serving bowl.

3 Stir in the tomato juice, a little at a time, then add a few drops of Worcestershire sauce and Tabasco sauce to taste. Mix well and set aside for 10–15 minutes.

4 Stir in the horseradish sauce and vodka. Squeeze the lemon and stir the juice into the salsa. Add salt and ground black pepper, to taste. Serve immediately, or cover and chill for 1–2 hours.

148 Salsas, Relishes and Dips

Roasted Tomato Salsa

Slow roasting these tomatoes to a semi-dried state results in a very rich, full-flavoured sweet sauce. The costeno amarillo chilli is mild and has a fresh light flavour, making it the perfect partner for the rich tomato taste. This salsa is great with tuna or sea bass and makes a marvellous sandwich filling when teamed with creamy cheese.

SERVES SIX AS AN ACCOMPANIMENT

INGREDIENTS

500g/1¼lb tomatoes
8 small shallots
5 garlic cloves
1 fresh rosemary sprig
2 costeno amarillo chillies
grated rind and juice of
 ½ small lemon
30ml/2 tbsp extra virgin olive oil
1.5ml/¼ tsp soft dark brown sugar
sea salt

1 Preheat the oven to 160°C/325°F/Gas 3. Cut the tomatoes into quarters and place them on a baking sheet.

2 Peel the shallots and garlic, and add them to the baking sheet. Sprinkle with sea salt. Roast in the oven for 1¼ hours or until the tomatoes are beginning to dry. If necessary, reduce the oven temperature to 150°C/300°F/Gas 2. Do not let the tomatoes burn or blacken or they will have a bitter taste.

3 Leave the tomatoes to cool, then peel off the skins and chop the flesh finely. Place in a bowl. Remove the outer layer of skin from any shallots that have toughened during cooking.

4 Using a large, sharp knife, chop the shallots and garlic roughly; place them with the tomatoes in a bowl and mix.

5 Strip the rosemary leaves from the woody stem and chop them finely. Add half to the tomato and shallot mixture and mix lightly.

6 Soak the chillies in hot water for about 10 minutes until soft. Drain, remove the stalks, slit them and scrape out the seeds with a sharp knife. Chop the flesh finely and add it to the tomato mixture. Mix well.

7 Stir in the lemon rind and juice, the olive oil and the sugar. Mix well, taste, and add more salt if needed. Cover and chill for at least 1 hour before serving, sprinkled with the remaining rosemary. The salsa will keep for up to 1 week in the refrigerator.

COOK'S TIP
Use plum tomatoes or vine tomatoes for this salsa – they have more flavour than tomatoes that have been grown for their keeping properties rather than their taste. Cherry tomatoes make delicious roasted tomato salsa; you can roast them whole, and there is no need to peel them after roasting.

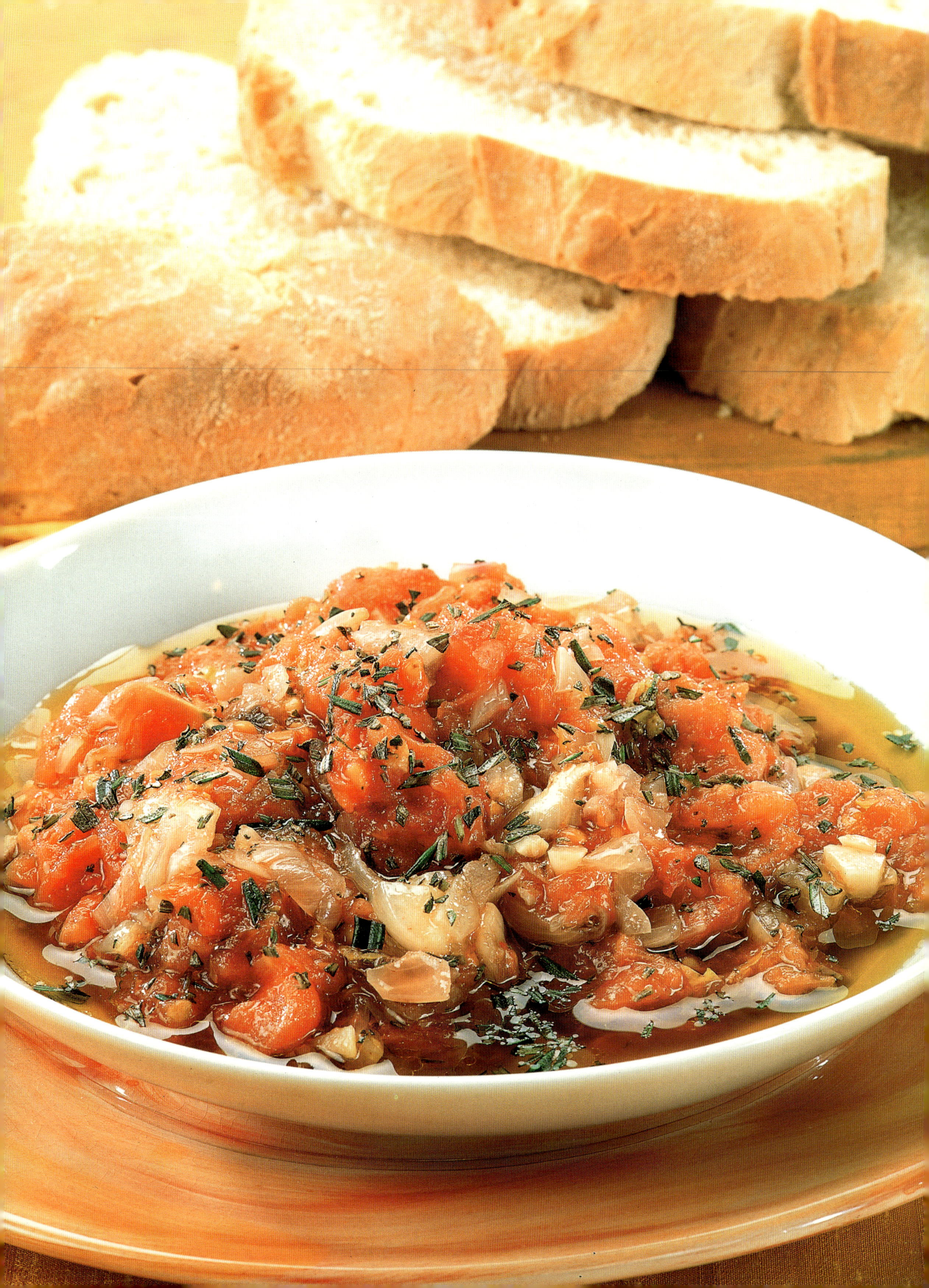

Apple and Tomato Chutney

THIS MELLOW, GOLDEN, SPICY CHUTNEY TRANSFORMS AN ORDINARY LUNCH INTO A REAL TREAT. ANY TYPE OF TOMATOES CAN BE USED SUCCESSFULLY IN THIS RECIPE.

MAKES ABOUT 1.8KG/4LB

INGREDIENTS
- 1.3kg/3lb cooking apples
- 1.3kg/3lb tomatoes
- 2 large onions, 2 garlic cloves
- 250g/9oz pitted dates
- 2 red (bell) peppers
- 3 dried red chillies
- 15ml/1 tbsp black peppercorns
- 4 cardamom pods
- 15ml/1 tbsp coriander seeds
- 10ml/2 tsp cumin seeds
- 10ml/2 tsp ground turmeric
- 15ml/1 tbsp salt
- 600ml/1 pint/2½ cups distilled malt vinegar
- 1kg/2¼lb/4½ cups granulated sugar

1 Peel and chop the apples. Peel and chop the tomatoes, onions and garlic. Quarter the dates. Core and seed the peppers, then cut into chunky pieces. Put all the prepared ingredients, except the red peppers, into a preserving pan.

2 Slit the chillies. Put the peppercorns and remaining spices into a mortar and roughly crush with a pestle. Add the chillies, spices and salt to the pan.

3 Pour in the vinegar and sugar. Leave to simmer for 30 minutes, stirring occasionally. Add the red pepper and cook for a further 30 minutes, stirring more frequently as the chutney becomes thick and pulpy.

4 Spoon into warm, dry, sterilized jars. Seal each jar with a waxed circle and cover with a tightly fitting cellophane top. Leave to cool.

Green Tomato Chutney

THIS IS A CLASSIC CHUTNEY TO MAKE AT THE END OF SUMMER WHEN THE LAST TOMATOES ON THE PLANTS IN THE GARDEN REFUSE TO RIPEN. LOOK OUT FOR GREEN TOMATOES ON MARKET STALLS, TOO.

MAKES ABOUT 2.5KG/5½LB

INGREDIENTS
   450g/1lb cooking apples
   1.8–2kg/4–4½lb green and red
      tomatoes, roughly chopped
   450g/1lb onions, chopped
   2 large garlic cloves, crushed
   15ml/1 tbsp salt
   45ml/3 tbsp pickling spice
   600ml/1 pint/2½ cups cider vinegar
   450g/1lb/2 cups sugar

1 Quarter the apples and use a sharp knife to remove the core from each piece. Remove the skin from the apples, then chop each wedge into small pieces.

2 Place the tomatoes, apples, onions and garlic in a preserving pan or a large, heavy pan. Add the salt. Tie the pickling spice in a piece of muslin (cheesecloth) and add it to the pan.

3 Pour in half the vinegar and bring to the boil. Lower the heat and simmer for 1 hour, or until the chutney is thick, stirring frequently.

4 Dissolve the sugar in the remaining vinegar and add to the chutney. Simmer for 1½ hours until the chutney is thick, stirring occasionally. Remove the muslin bag from the chutney.

5 Spoon the hot chutney into warm, sterilized jars. Seal each jar with a waxed circle and cover with a tightly fitting cellophane top. Store in a cool, dark place for at least 1 month before using.

COOK'S TIPS
• To make it easier to retrieve the muslin bag filled with pickling spice, tie it with a piece of string to the handle of the pan.
• Use a jam funnel to transfer the chutney into the jars. Wipe the jars and label them when cold.

Tomato and Red Pepper Relish

This spicy relish will keep for at least a week in the refrigerator. It is particularly good with sausages and burgers, but also makes a great accompaniment for a mature Cheddar.

SERVES EIGHT

INGREDIENTS
- 1 onion
- 1 red (bell) pepper, seeded
- 2 garlic cloves
- 6 tomatoes
- 30ml/2 tbsp extra virgin olive oil or sunflower oil
- 5ml/1 tsp ground cinnamon
- about 5ml/1 tsp chilli flakes
- 5ml/1 tsp ground ginger
- 5ml/1 tsp salt
- 2.5ml/½ tsp ground black pepper
- 75g/3oz/⅓ cup light brown sugar, or other dark sugar
- 75ml/5 tbsp cider vinegar
- handful of fresh basil leaves

COOK'S TIPS
- This relish thickens slightly on cooling so do not worry if the mixture seems a little thin after being simmered for 20 minutes.
- The precise amount of chilli flakes added depends upon personal taste. Chillies can be omitted entirely, if a milder taste is preferred. On the other hand, the chilli flavour can be intensified, either by adding more flakes, or by substituting 1–2 chopped fresh chillies for the red pepper.

1 Put the tomatoes in a heatproof bowl. Boil some water in a kettle or pan and then pour it over the tomatoes. Leave for 30 seconds. Remove the tomatoes with a slotted spoon and cool in cold water. Drain well.

2 Using a small, sharp knife, scrape and peel off the skins from each tomato in turn. They should slip off fairly easily, but you may need to slice off the skin if it sticks. Chop the tomatoes.

3 Chop the onion, pepper and garlic. Gently heat the oil in a pan. Add the onion, pepper and garlic to the pan.

4 Cook gently for 5–8 minutes, until the pepper has softened, but still retains its shape. Add the chopped tomatoes. Cover and cook for 5 minutes, stirring often, until the tomatoes release their juices.

5 Stir in the cinnamon, chilli flakes, ginger, salt, pepper, sugar and vinegar. Bring to the boil over a low heat, stirring constantly until all the sugar has dissolved.

6 Simmer the relish mixture, uncovered, for 20 minutes, until it becomes pulpy. Stir in the basil leaves and check the seasoning.

7 Allow the relish to cool completely, then transfer it to a glass jar or a plastic container with a tightly fitting lid. Cover tightly, label if necessary and store in the refrigerator.

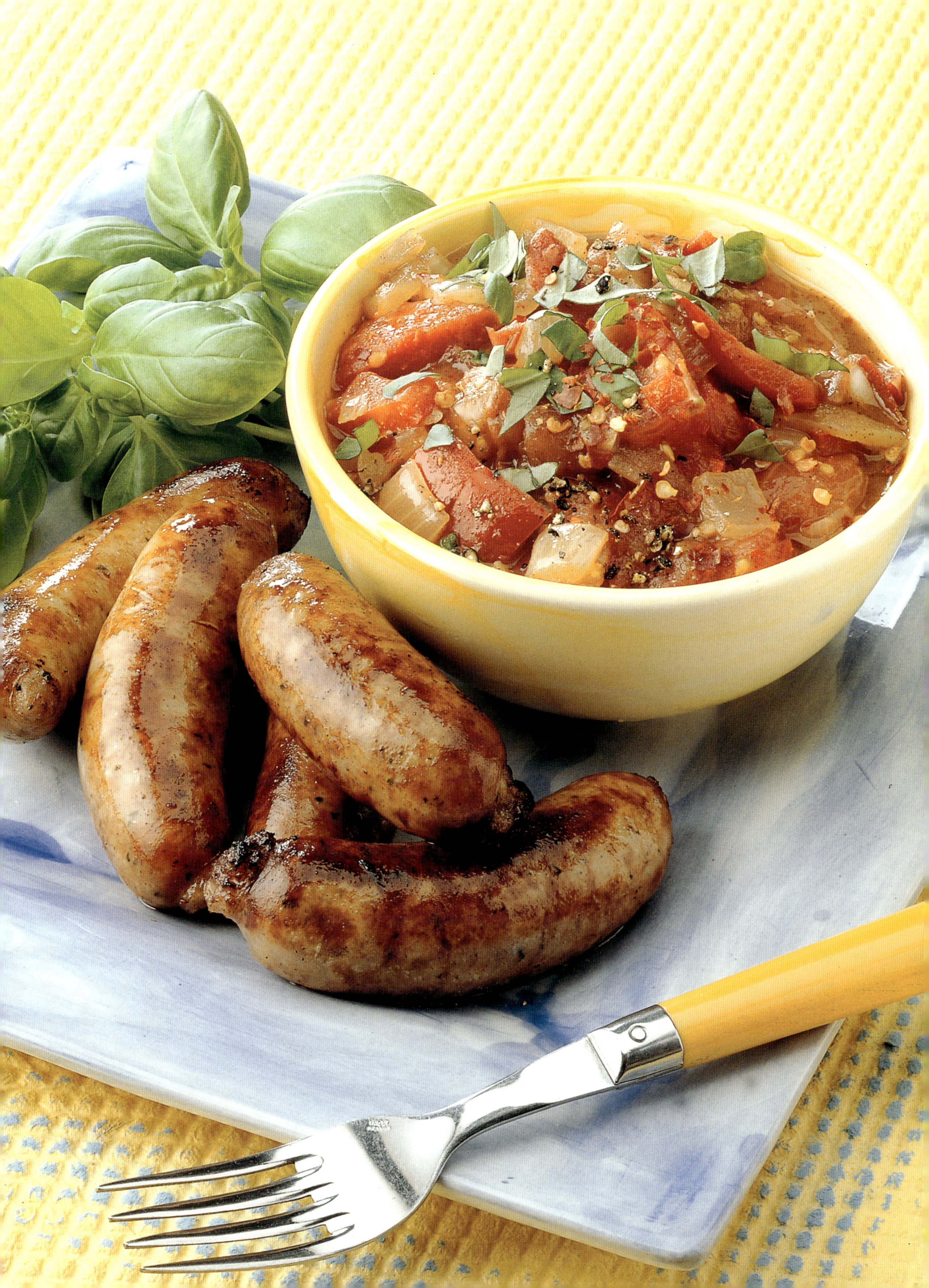

Aromatic Guacamole

GUACAMOLE IS OFTEN SERVED AS A FIRST COURSE WITH CORN CHIPS FOR DIPPING. THIS CHUNKY VERSION IS A GREAT ACCOMPANIMENT FOR GRILLED FISH, POULTRY OR MEAT, ESPECIALLY STEAK.

SERVES FOUR

INGREDIENTS
- 2 large ripe avocados
- 1 small red onion, very finely chopped
- 1 red or green chilli, seeded and very finely chopped
- ½–1 garlic clove, crushed with a little salt
- finely grated rind of ½ lime and juice of 1–1½ limes
- pinch of sugar
- 225g/8oz tomatoes, seeded and chopped
- 30ml/2 tbsp roughly chopped fresh coriander (cilantro)
- 2.5–5ml/½–1 tsp ground toasted cumin seeds
- 15ml/1 tbsp olive oil
- 15–30ml/1–2 tbsp sour cream (optional)
- salt and ground black pepper
- lime wedges dipped in sea salt, and fresh coriander (cilantro) sprigs, to garnish

1 Cut 1 avocado in half and lift out and discard the stone (pit). Scrape the flesh from both halves into a bowl and mash it roughly with a fork.

2 Stir in the onion, chilli, garlic, lime rind, sugar, tomatoes and coriander. Add the ground cumin and seasoning to taste, then stir in the olive oil.

3 Halve and stone (pit) the remaining avocado. Dice the flesh and stir it into the guacamole.

4 Squeeze in fresh lime juice to taste, mix well, then cover and leave to stand for 15 minutes so that the flavour develops. Stir in the sour cream, if using. Serve with lime wedges dipped in sea salt, and fresh coriander sprigs.

COOK'S TIP
To crush garlic, place a peeled clove on a chopping board and chop it roughly. Sprinkle over a little sea salt and, using the flat side of a large knife blade, gradually work the salt into the garlic.

Salsas, Relishes and Dips 155

Sour Cream Dip

This cooling tomato and pepper dip is a perfect accompaniment to hot and spicy dishes. Alternatively, serve it as a snack with the fieriest tortilla chips you can find.

SERVES TWO

INGREDIENTS
 1 small yellow (bell) pepper
 2 tomatoes
 30ml/2 tbsp chopped fresh parsley
 150ml/¼ pint/⅔ cup sour cream
 grated lemon rind,
  to garnish

VARIATIONS
• Vary the colour combinations by using yellow, orange or red peppers with red or yellow tomatoes. Green pepper with yellow tomatoes looks good with the chopped parsley.
• Use Greek (US strained plain) yogurt or crème fraîche instead of sour cream.
• Use finely diced avocado or cucumber in place of the pepper.

1 Halve the pepper lengthways. Remove the core and seeds, then cut the flesh into tiny dice.

2 Halve the tomatoes, then scoop out and discard the seeds and cut the flesh into tiny dice.

3 Stir the pepper and tomato dice and the chopped parsley into the sour cream and mix well.

4 Spoon the dip into a small bowl and chill. Garnish by sprinkling with grated lemon rind before serving.

Thousand Island Dip

This variation on the classic Thousand Island Dressing is far removed from the original version, but can be served in the same way — with shellfish laced on to bamboo skewers for dipping or with a simple mixed salad.

SERVES FOUR

INGREDIENTS
4 sun-dried tomatoes in oil
4 plum tomatoes, or
    2 beefsteak tomatoes
150g/5oz/⅔ cup mild soft cheese, or
    mascarpone or fromage frais
60ml/4 tbsp mayonnaise
30ml/2 tbsp tomato purée (paste)
30ml/2 tbsp chopped fresh parsley
1 lemon
Tabasco sauce, to taste
5ml/1 tsp Worcestershire sauce or
    soy sauce
salt and ground black pepper

COOK'S TIP
Tabasco sauce packs quite a punch, so use it with care. Add just a couple of drops at first, beat it in and leave for a minute or so to allow the flavour to develop. Taste the dip and add more Tabasco if needed. Continue this process until you feel it has the correct amount of flavouring.

1 Use a slotted spoon to scoop the sun-dried tomatoes out of the jar and place them on a double sheet of kitchen paper to absorb the excess oil. Blot them all over with the paper.

2 Transfer them to a chopping board and check that the stalk and blossom ends of each tomato have been removed; if not, trim them and then cut the sun-dried tomatoes into small pieces.

3 Cut a cross in the base of each fresh tomato. Bring a small pan of water to the boil. Remove it from the heat and add the tomatoes. Leave for 30 seconds, then lift the tomatoes out with a slotted spoon and put them into a bowl of cold water. Drain. The skin will have begun to peel back from the crosses. Remove it, then cut the tomatoes in half and squeeze out the seeds. Chop the flesh finely.

4 Put the soft cheese in a bowl. Beat it until it is creamy, then gradually beat in the mayonnaise. Add the tomato purée in the same way.

VARIATIONS
• Stir in 2.5ml/½ tsp cayenne pepper or a chopped fresh chilli for a fiery dip.
• To add a more exotic flavour to this dip, you can vary the ingredients slightly – try using freshly squeezed lime juice instead of lemon juice, and swap the parsley for a few sprigs of aromatic coriander (cilantro) or try orange juice and very finely chopped lemon grass.

5 Stir in the parsley and sun-dried tomatoes, then the fresh tomatoes. Mix well so that the dip is evenly coloured.

6 Grate the lemon rind finely and add it to the dip. Mix well. Squeeze the lemon and add the juice to the bowl, with Tabasco sauce to taste. Stir in the Worcestershire sauce or soy sauce, and salt and pepper to taste.

7 Spoon the dip into a serving bowl, swirling the surface attractively. Cover with clear film and chill in the refrigerator until ready to serve.

INDEX

A

aubergines: Moussaka 80
    Scrambled Eggs 44
avocados: Aromatic Guacamole 154
    Avocado, Tomato and Orange Salad 67
    Bean Feast with Tomato and Avocado Salsa 127
    Tomato Rice and Beans with Avocado Salsa 132

B

Baked Tomatoes Provençal Style 60
basil 20
    Chilled Tomato and Basil-flower Soup 33
    Roasted Tomato and Mozzarella with Basil Oil and Mixed Leaf Salad 46
    Tomato and Basil Tart 138
    Tomato and Fresh Basil Soup 34
bay 20
beef: Beef and Lentil Balls with Tomato Sauce 82
    Beef Stew with Red Wine and Peas 84
    Tagliatelle with Bolognese Sauce 85
beefsteak tomatoes 10, 12, 13, 15, 23, 25
bread: Cannellini Bean and Tomato Bruschetta 48
    Mozzarella and Tomato Skewers 50
    Pipérade with Crostini 49
    Tomato Bread and Butter Bake 116
bushes 10, 11, 26

C

canned tomatoes 8, 19
Cassoulet 86
cheese *see* individual types of cheese
cherry tomatoes 9, 12, 13, 15
    bottled tomatoes 18
    Bulgur Wheat and Cherry Tomato Salad 66
    Roasted Cherry Tomato, Pasta and Rocket Salad 74
    Spicy Tuna, Chickpea and Cherry Tomato Salad 72
chicken: Chicken Khoresh 92
    Chicken with Chorizo 90
    Varna-style Chicken 91
chillies 20
chives 20
    Orange, Tomato and Chive Salsa 144
chutneys: Apple and Tomato Chutney 150
    Green Tomato Chutney 151
cilantro *see* coriander
cinnamon 20
cod: Baked Cod with Tomatoes and Peppers 97
    Mexican-style Salt Cod 98
    Roasted Cod with Fresh Tomato Sauce 96
coldhouses 8, 9
concassing 16
cordons 10, 11, 13, 26
coriander 20
    Okra with Coriander and Tomatoes 54
Corn: Mushroom, and Plum Tomato Wholewheat Pizza 140
courgettes: Courgettes in Tomato Sauce 58
    Ribollita 37
    Tomato and Vegetable Bake 60
couscous: Couscous with Eggs and Tomato Sauce 128
    Hot Vegetable Couscous with Harissa 129
cream cheese: Tomato and Cheese Tarts 45
creamed tomatoes 19
crêpes: Baked Herb Crêpes with Tomato Sauce 123
cultivation 10–11
cutting tomatoes 16

D

dips: Sour Cream Dip 155
    Thousand Island Dip 156
diseases of tomatoes 11
drying and preserving in oil 18

E

eggplant *see* aubergines
eggs: Couscous with Eggs and Tomato Sauce 128
    Pipérade with Crostini 49
    Scrambled Eggs 44
equipment 14–15

F

Fattoush 62
fennel: Grilled Leek and Fennel Salad with Spicy Tomato Dressing 68
fertilizer 10, 11
feta cheese: Turkish Tomato Salad 64
fish: Brodetto 104
    Caribbean Fish Steaks 108
    Fish Boulettes on Hot Tomato Sauce 105
    Mediterranean Fish Cutlets with Aniseed Tomato Sauce 106
    Mediterranean Leek and Fish Soup with Tomatoes and Garlic 43
    Provençal Fish Soup 42
    Seafood Soup with Rouille 40
    see also cod; monkfish; red snapper; swordfish; tuna
flame-skinning tomatoes 16
freezing 18

G

garlic 20
    Mediterranean Leek and Fish Soup with Tomatoes and Garlic 43
    Roasted Garlic and Butternut Squash Soup with Tomato Salsa 35
    Roasted Plum Tomatoes with Garlic 56
ginger: Potato Rösti and Tofu with Fresh Tomato and Ginger Sauce 120
glasshouses 6, 7, 8–9, 10, 11
green tomatoes 13
    Green Tomato Chutney 151
greenhouses 10–11
grow bags 10, 11
Gruyère cheese: Baked Cheese Polenta with Tomato Sauce 114
Guacamole, Aromatic 154

H

hanging baskets 11, 26, 28
harissa: Hot Vegetable Couscous with Harissa 129
heirloom tomatoes 26, 27, 29
heritage tomatoes *see* heirloom tomatoes
history of tomatoes 6–8
hybrid tomatoes 8, 12, 22

L

lamb: Greek Lamb Sausages with Tomato Sauce 78
    Lamb Burgers with Hot, Spicy Red Onion and Tomato Relish 79
    Moroccan Harira 39
    Moussaka 80

Lancashire cheese: Cheese Sausages with Tomato Sauce 122
leeks: Cheese and Leek Sausages with Hot Tomato Sauce 122
　Grilled Leek and Fennel Salad with Spicy Tomato Dressing 68
　Leek, Squash and Tomato Gratin 115
　Mediterranean Leek and Fish Soup with Tomatoes and Garlic 43
lentils: Beef and Lentil Balls with Tomato Sauce 82
　Harvest Vegetable and Lentil Casserole 117
　Tomato and Lentil Dhal with Almonds 126

M
mace 20
marjoram 21
mint 20
Monkfish with Tomatoes 107
mouli 14
mozzarella cheese: Mozzarella and Tomato Skewers 50
　Roasted Tomato and Mozzarella with Basil Oil and Mixed Leaf Salad 46
mushrooms: Mushroom, Corn and Plum Tomato Wholewheat Pizza 140
　Rigatoni with Tomatoes, Wild Mushrooms and Fresh Herbs 135

N
nutmeg 20
nutrition 8, 9–10

O
Okra with Coriander and Tomatoes 54
orange tomatoes 13
oranges: Avocado, Tomato and Orange Salad 67
　Orange, Tomato and Chive Salsa 144
oregano 21

P
paprika 20
parsley 21
passata 19
pasta: Black Pasta with Squid and Tomato Sauce 109
　Borlotti Bean and Pasta Soup 38
　Country Pasta Salad 75
　Paglia e Fieno with Sun-dried Tomatoes and Radicchio 134
　Pasta with Tomato and Chilli Sauce 133
　Pasta with Tomatoes and Shellfish 113
　Rigatoni with Tomatoes, Wild Mushrooms and Fresh Herbs 135
　Tagliatelle with Bolognese Sauce 85
　Tortiglioni with Spicy Sausage Sauce 88
pear tomatoes 13
peeling tomatoes 16
peppers: Roasted Peppers with Tomatoes 57
　Stuffed Beefsteak Tomatoes and Red and Yellow Peppers 125
　Tomato and Red Pepper Relish 152
pesto, red 19
pests 8, 9, 11
pinching out 10, 11
pizzas: Classic Marinara Pizza 141
　Hot Pepperoni Pizza 89
　Mushroom, Corn and Plum Tomato Wholewheat Pizza 140
plum tomatoes 12, 13, 19
　Mushroom, Corn and Plum Tomato Wholewheat Pizza 140
　Roasted Plum Tomatoes with Garlic 56
polenta: Baked Cheese Polenta with Tomato Sauce 114
　Herby Polenta with Tomatoes 47
potatoes: Marquis Potatoes 55
　Potato Gnocchi with Simple Tomato and Butter Sauce 118
　Potato Rösti and Tofu with Fresh Tomato and Ginger Sauce 120
prawns: Ceviche 101
　Grilled King Prawns with Romesco Sauce 110
　Pasta with Tomatoes and Shellfish 113
　Provençal Fish Soup 42
　Seafood Soup with Rouille 40
preparing tomatoes 16–17
preserving tomatoes 18
purées 14, 19

R
Red Snapper Burritos with Chilli and Cheese 102
relish: Tomato and Red Pepper Relish 152
rice: Mexican Rice 130
　Provençal Fish Soup 42
　Tomato Rice 131
　Tomato Rice and Beans with Avocado Salsa 132
ripening 9, 10, 11, 12, 13
rosemary 21

S
saffron: Hot Vegetable Couscous with Tomatoes and Harissa 129
sage 21
salad tomatoes 12, 13
salads: Avocado, Tomato and Orange Salad 67
　Black Olive, Tomato and Sardine Salad 70
　Bulgur Wheat and Cherry Tomato Salad 66
　Country Pasta Salad with Fresh Cherry Tomatoes 75
　Cucumber and Tomato Salad 70
　Fattoush 62
　Grilled Leek and Fennel Salad with Spicy Tomato Dressing 68
　Mango, Tomato and Red Onion Salad 63
　Persian Salad with Tomatoes 64
　Roasted Cherry Tomato, Pasta and Rocket Salad 74
　Roasted Tomato and Mozzarella with Basil Oil and Mixed Leaf Salad 46
　Smoked Bacon and Tomato Salad with Pasta Twists 73
　Spicy Tuna, Chickpea and Cherry Tomato Salad 72
　Turkish Tomato Salad 64
salsas: Aromatic Guacamole 154
　Bean Feast with Tomato and Avocado Salsa 127
　Bloody Mary Salsa 147
　Fiery Salsa 146
　Orange, Tomato and Chive Salsa 144
　Roasted Tomato Salsa 148
　Smoky Tomato Salsa 145
　Tostadas with Tomato Salsa 51

sardines: Black Olive, Tomato and
    Sardine Salad 70
sausages: Cassoulet 86
    Cheese and Leek Sausages with
        Hot Tomato Sauce 122
    Chicken with Chorizo 90
    Greek Lamb Sausages with Tomato
        Sauce 78
    Tortiglioni with Spicy Sausage
        Sauce 88
seeding tomatoes 16
seedlings 10
semi-bush tomatoes 26
shrimp see prawns
side shoots 10, 11
soups: Borlotti Bean and Pasta
        Soup 38
    Chilled Tomato and Basil-flower
        Soup 33
    Iced Tomato and Vodka Soup 32
    Mediterranean Leek and Fish Soup with
        Tomatoes and Garlic 43
    Moroccan Harira 39
    Pistou 36
    Provençal Fish Soup 42
    Ribollita 37
    Roasted Garlic and Butternut Squash
        Soup with Tomato Salsa 35
    Seafood Soup with Rouille 40

Tomato and Fresh Basil Soup 34
sowing seeds 10, 11
spices 20, 21
    see also individual spices
spinach: Spiced Turnips with Spinach
    and Tomatoes 59
squash: Leek, Squash and Tomato
    Gratin 115
    Roasted Garlic and Butternut Squash
        Soup with Tomato Salsa 35
squid: Black Pasta with Squid and Tomato
    Sauce 109
    Ceviche 101
store-cupboard tomatoes 19
sugocasa 19
sun-ripening 12
support 10, 26
swordfish: Chargrilled Swordfish with
    Spicy Tomato and Lime
    Sauce 100

T
thyme 21
tofu: Potato Rösti and Tofu with Fresh
    Tomato and Ginger Sauce 120
tomato fans 17
tomato ketchup 18
tomato lilies 17
tomato purée 14, 19

tomato roses 17
    Spicy Tomato Tart with Tomato
        Roses 139
tomato suns 17
Tortilla Parcels, Mexican 124
tuna: Fresh Tuna and Tomato
    Stew 103
    Spicy Tuna, Chickpea and Cherry
        Tomato Salad 72
Turkey and Tomato Meatballs 93
Turkish Tomato Salad 64
turnips: Spiced Turnips with Spinach
    and Tomatoes 59

V
varieties 7, 8, 10, 12, 22–29
    see also individual types
Vegetable Tarte Tatin 136
vine tomatoes 9, 13

W
watering 8, 10, 11
winter savory 21

Y
yellow tomatoes 13

Z
zucchini see courgettes

ACKNOWLEDGEMENTS AND SUPPLIERS

The author and publisher would like to thank Jim Buckland and Sarah Wain of West Dean Gardens for their generous assistance. Many of the varieties of tomato photographed came from their gardens, which are open to the public. They host a tomato show in September every year. For recorded information on opening times and charges for the gardens, tel. 00 44 (0) 1243 818210 or write to West Dean Gardens, West Dean, Chichester, West Sussex, PO18 0QZ, UK.

Totally Tomatoes, PO Box 202, Newton Abbot, TQ12 6ZH, UK, tel. 00 44 (0) 1803 389516, is an excellent source of tomato seeds in the UK, carrying more than 200 varieties from all over the world. Their website is www.totallytomatouk.com. Simpson's Seeds, run by Colin, Jane and Matt Simpson, is a supplier, specializing in the most flavoursome varieties. Selling plants and seeds by mail order, the address is 27 Meadowbrook, Old Oxted, Surrey, RH8 9LT, UK, tel. 00 44 (0) 13 715242. Another good source of seeds in the UK is E W King & Co Ltd, Monk's Farm, Kelvedon, Colchester, Essex, CO5 9PG, UK, telephone 00 44 (0) 1376 570000. For rare varieties, contact Ferme de Sainte Marthe at PO Box 358, Walton, Surrey KT12 4YX, tel. 00 44 (0) 1932 266630. For US readers, heirloom tomato seeds can be supplied by The Cook's Garden, PO Box 5010, Hodges, SC 29653, USA, tel. 001 (0) 800 457 9703, or www.cooksgarden.com. Also Seed Savers Exchange, 3076 North Winn Road, Decorah, IA 52101, USA, telephone: 00 1 (0) 319 382 5990. Their website is www.seedsavers.com. Another company supplying seeds is Heirloom Seeds, PO Box 245, West Elizabeth, PA 15088, USA, tel. 00 1 (0) 412 384 0852 or www.heirloomseeds.com.

Lakeland Limited, Alexandra Buildings, Windermere, Cumbria, LA23 1BQ, UK, www.lakelandlimited.com, is a good source of equipment.

Picture Acknowledgements
The Art Archive: p6 both, p7 both; Cephas: p8 top.